Fill Your Tank With Freedom

Klassy Evans
& Adam Khan

Published by: Free Woman Press
Printed in the United States

Fill Your Tank With Freedom © Copyright 2012
Klassy Evans and Adam Khan, all rights reserved.

ISBN-13: 978-1623815011
ISBN-10: 1623815010

Visit our web site, sign up for free updates, and contact
us here:

FillYourTankWithFreedom.com

Dedication

To the millions of women throughout the world
who live without the basic rights and freedoms
we take for granted in the United States.

Table of Contents

Acknowledgments

We'd like to thank Anne Korin, Gal Luft, and Robert Zubrin for clarifying our urgent need for fuel competition. We'd also like to thank Andy Miller, Lisa Piraneo and Kelly Cook for their support and encouragement.

The Transportation Economy

Every American president since Nixon has been concerned about America's dependence on oil and the high price of gasoline, and they've all wanted to do something about it.

The problem is, we *need* oil. Our economy completely depends on it. The U.S. economy slows or grows as the price of oil goes up and down. And yet we know our dependence on petroleum is dangerous.

In this book, we're going to explore how we got ourselves into our precarious situation and what we can do to get out — what we can do as a nation, and what we can each do personally.

The most immediate solution to our dilemma is to use alcohol to fuel our cars. Alcohol fuels (methanol, ethanol, butanol, and propanol) don't have to completely replace oil to solve our problem, they only have to comprise a large enough percentage to give petroleum fuels real competition.

The competition will lower gas prices, but it will also have many other positive effects. A thriving alcohol industry will add millions of American jobs; it will revitalize our economy by pouring more of our money into our own industries; it will reduce the amount of pollution and CO_2 released into the air; it will greatly improve our national security without spending any more money; and it will prevent future oil shocks and the recessions they cause.

Alcohol is also a cleaner fuel that burns cooler, so it increases the life of car engines.

As I'm writing this, regular gasoline is over four dollars a gallon. And yet today some people are using a clean, completely renewable, homegrown fuel that only costs them about a dollar a gallon.

You will find out later in this book how you can be among the early adopters of this fuel revolution. America may be dependent on foreign oil now, but we can become independent, and fairly quickly, as you'll soon discover. But first, let's take a hard look at our situation and how we got here.

The Situation As It Is

The world is being robbed. Today billions of dollars will leave the free world and go to OPEC (Organization of the Petroleum Exporting Countries), a cartel that controls 78% of the world's proven oil reserves. The oil produced by the OPEC nations adds up to such a large percentage of total world production (about 42%) that OPEC can determine the global price of oil (by collectively deciding how much oil they will produce). And they deliberately restrain their production to keep the price of oil high.

OPEC was founded in 1960 by Iran, Iraq, Kuwait, Saudi Arabia and Venezuela. Since then, Qatar, Libya, the United Arab Emirates, Algeria, Nigeria, Angola, and Ecuador have become members of OPEC. The reason they founded OPEC was to raise global oil prices (and thus make more money).

These twelve oil-producing nations set the world price of oil by meeting at least twice a year and deciding what their combined production ceiling will be.

OPEC has teams of people who study world oil demand and calculate how much to restrain production to create the price they're aiming for, taking into account the bidding wars that will ensue when oil becomes even slightly scarcer in relation to the existing demand.

While we have been struggling to endure a worldwide recession, *billions* of dollars flowed out of the free world into OPEC bank accounts *this week*. It'll happen again next week. And the week after.

Last year alone, over a *trillion* dollars left the free world's economy and made its way to OPEC nations, and it is projected to be even more this year. OPEC is siphoning off this almost unimaginable amount of money by price fixing, *and it is illegal.*

Conspiring to fix prices is a crime according to U.S. law, but it's also a crime according to international law. The World Trade Organization has established antitrust rules against member nations setting "quota restrictions" on their imports and exports in order to manipulate prices, and it allows for the prosecution of illegal collusion among nations.

The U.S. Justice Department would be legally justified in prosecuting OPEC executive officers and owners who have interests in the U.S. (like Saudi oil billionaires) for conspiring to fix prices. And it would be legal to prosecute *any* organization participating in the OPEC scheme — international oil companies, for example.

The member nations of the World Trade Organization could also legally enforce trade-restriction retaliation procedures against OPEC nations.

None of this is likely to happen, however. Why? OPEC could (and probably would) respond with an even worse oil embargo than the one in 1973 that crippled America's economy (and much of the free world's economy) for *years*.

So no government that relies on foreign oil is foolish enough to prosecute OPEC for their illegal, unethical, and dangerous cartel.

OPEC is running the most powerful monopoly on earth with the number one strategic commodity on earth, which gave it the power to *double* the price of oil in only two years during the worst recession of our lifetimes. They deliberately voted to *cut back* their production, so the price went up (as they knew it would) and everyone with a gas-only engine paid the price because we had no choice about it.

This is monumental. We are witnessing the largest transfer of wealth in the history of the world. The free world is giving immense sums of money to OPEC nations. And the United States — the largest *consumer*

4

of oil in the world — is helping pour money into Saudi Arabia — the largest *producer* of oil in the world. And the sums are continually rising, as OPEC keeps pushing the price higher.

This is having two major effects that are important to Americans: The U.S. economy is struggling to rise out of a recession; *and* dangerous men and dangerous regimes are accumulating an alarming degree of power because of their wealth.

The Economic Impact

Oil has been the foundation of the American economy for a hundred years, and it remains so today. When anything is sold, it usually has to first travel — by car, plane, train, ship, or truck, and often all of these. Goods are loaded onto a ship, and when they arrive in America the containers are loaded onto a train and taken to a central distribution point where they are loaded onto trucks and then delivered to a store, where you and I buy it and drive it home in our cars. The ship, the train, the truck and your own car are all likely to be designed and warranted to burn nothing but petroleum.

The world's trade network (and therefore the world's economy) relies on shipping goods from place to place. And within the United States, 97 percent of these transportation vehicles *can burn nothing but petroleum*. Worldwide, 95 percent of *all* transportation vehicles can burn nothing but petroleum. So when the world price of oil goes up, the price of *everything* goes up all over the world.

The price of oil even impacts the price of goods produced and sold locally. For example, most farmers use equipment that burns petroleum. Fuel is a major expense of theirs. Not only do tractors use petroleum, but fertilizers, pesticides, and herbicides are usually made from petroleum.

So when oil prices go up, the prices of all agricultural products go up, which means grain prices go up, which means the price of animal feed goes up, which means the price of eggs, chicken, poultry, milk, cheese, and beef goes up too.

Much of the cost of packaged food is in the packaging itself — the plastic wrapping, which is usually made from petroleum, and the ink on the outside of the box is usually made from petroleum too.

And, of course, many products *themselves* are made with a good deal of plastic.

So when oil prices rise, the price of almost *everything* else rises, and the world's economic vitality goes down.

The Elephant on Our Back

In a memorable scene from the movie, *Apollo 13*, two pilots are trying to manually aim their spacecraft toward the earth, and struggling to do so.

Jim Lovell says to ground control, "We're all out of whack. We try to pitch down but we yaw to the left. Why can't I null this out?"

Fred Haise says to Lovell, "She wasn't designed to fly attached like this. Our center of gravity is the command module."

Lovell says, "It's like flying with a dead elephant on our back."

I just saw a headline that reminded me of that last line: "Recovery Stalls as Gas Prices Rise." The U.S. is struggling to "null this out." We are trying to recover from a deep recession but it's like flying with a dead elephant on our back.

The elephant is OPEC. Quoting from the article (from TimesUnion.com):

"Rising gas prices take billions of dollars out of consumers' pockets without producing any noticeable benefit for the economy. State Comptroller Thomas DiNapoli estimates that a typical New Yorker will pay more than $1,800 more a year for gasoline and heating oil alone than just two years ago if prices don't ease. That doesn't include the increased prices for food and other goods that higher energy costs mean.

"This kind of spending doesn't create jobs; it simply siphons off money. The Union of Concerned Scientists estimates that at $100 a barrel for oil, about $1 billion leaves the U.S. economy every day to pay for petroleum imports. That's equivalent to more than half of the U.S. trade deficit."

In 2007, the price of petroleum was $70 a barrel. OPEC restricted its oil production, so the price of oil climbed to $140 per barrel and then the economy tanked. Many people said the economic collapse was because of "speculative mortgage-backed securities" which lost their value when the housing market collapsed.

But, asks Robert Zubrin, author of *Energy Victory*, "Why did the global housing market collapse?" Because people ran low on money all over the world. But why? Where was everyone's money?

It went to pay for oil.

In 2008, Americans forked over $900 billion for oil (the total cost of all the oil purchased in the world that year was $3.6 trillion). This amount of money was "up by a factor of ten" from what it was in 1999. As Zubrin describes it, this rising cost represents "a huge, highly regressive tax on the world economy."

And it continues to increase. Americans paid $80 billion for oil in 1999 and they paid $900 billion ten years later. This is equivalent to a "33 percent increase in income taxes across the board." And 60 percent of that money was handed over to foreign governments.

In an interview with Eyal Aronoff, co-founder of the Fuel Freedom Foundation, he said, "The people that pay the high price for gasoline are disproportionately the lower middle class…The price of fuel you pay is proportional to the distance that you can drive, because your income is stable, and it is a proxy to your employment opportunity."

As the cost of fuel rises, you must find employment closer to home. Think about where the lower middle class lives. They can't afford to live close to where they work because the cost of housing is too high there. So they are being priced out of the employment market. "And that is partly why we are seeing such high unemployment," says Aronoff. "So as the price of gasoline rises, we have more and more disenfranchised people in our community, and that takes an incredible social toll, not to mention that it could reignite a whole new set of mortgage defaults, which can destabilize banks again. Which is exactly what happened to us last go round — when the price of oil spiked, the banks went under. Of course there were many other reasons. But this was the big trigger."

So the housing bubble created a precarious situation for many Americans. They may have been in over their heads, but they were squeaking by. Rising gas prices, however (transportation is the second biggest expense for most people behind housing itself), pushed them over the cliff. They didn't have much give in their budgets because of their house payments, and when gas prices climbed steeply and suddenly, they did not have enough money to pay their mortgages.

With fuel competition, these kinds of destructive price hikes would no longer occur. And if the money we spent on fuel was buying a fuel made in America (at a price controlled by the free market rather than OPEC), it would save us money, generate jobs, and help our economy.

But instead, in the last ten years, roughly half the money we spent for transportation fuel left our country. And even though our own domestic drilling is increasing, the amount we send out of the country is still increasing because of rising prices.

There is another insidious side effect of rising gasoline prices. As people spend more money on gas, they spend less money on other things, *and that causes the loss of jobs.* "Since consumer spending is the main driver of the U.S. economy," says Mark Cooper, Research Director of the Consumer Federation of America, "when speculators, oil companies and OPEC rob consumers of that much spending power, the inevitable result is a dramatic reduction of economic activity and employment."

In Cooper's study of the effect of oil prices on jobs, he discovered that *every time* oil prices have spiked since World War II, we've had a recession in America. In his study, he showed that because oil was about $30 a barrel higher than "costs or historic trends justify," gas prices rose by a dollar a gallon in one year (from the summer of 2010 to the summer of 2011), which drained about 200 billion dollars from the economy. This is about two percent of consumer spending. That doesn't seem like much, but two percent less spending (200 billion dollars) created the loss of *hundreds of thousands* of jobs.

Another way to look at it is that because most of our cars are not warranted to burn anything but gasoline, we imported about $500 billion dollars per year of oil, sending that money out of the country. That would have paid *five million* workers $100,000 a year! Since the average American salary is less than a third of that, we can easily say it would have paid the salaries of *fifteen million* Americans.

But the money leaving our country just leaves — doing nothing for us. If the same money was paid to workers here, it would have a huge ripple effect in our economy because that money would then be used to buy other goods and services in America.

Rising Oil Bill

In 1972, America spent $4 billion for imported oil. At that time, $4 billion was 1.2% of our defense budget, just to give you a price to compare it to. America traditionally spends a good deal of money on its defense.

In 1999, we paid about $40 billion to import oil, which was 15% of our defense budget. The trend is a dangerous upward curve. By 2006, we paid $260 billion, which was 50% of our defense budget. The very next year, it went up to $342 billion, which was almost 70% of our defense budget.

The following year, it went over the 100% mark. We imported 650 billion dollars worth of oil, which was 130% of our defense budget. The price per barrel keeps rising.

The wealth flooding into OPEC nations has, of course, grown in proportion to the rising price of oil. These countries are, by and large, kingdoms and dictatorships, so the tremendous wealth is accumulating in the hands of very few people.

What are they doing with it?

Since Saudi Arabia *has* more oil than any other country, and their oil is the cheapest to produce, and even after restraining their output, they still *produce* more oil by far than any other country, many of these superwealthy men are Saudi princes who use their money to promote Wahhabi Islam, a virulent fundamentalist movement. Wahhabi princes fund madrassas all over the world. These schools teach nothing but fundamentalist Islam to poor Muslim boys who come for the free food and are taught to hate non-Muslims, to treat women as second-class citizens, and that the way to Paradise is to die while fighting non-Muslims. They do not teach these boys employable skills. They graduate qualified to be a jihadist and little else.

Wahhabi-controlled oil money is also being used to build and buy (and control) mosques all over the world — including in America — mosques that do the same thing: Promote misogyny, hatred of non-Muslims, and the political imperative to undermine and eventually overthrow democracies and replace the existing laws with Islamic law.

Even in America, the majority of the mosques teach these things. In 2005, the Center for Religious Freedom found widespread distribution of intolerant jihadist material in American mosques. In testimony before the U.S. State Department in 1999, Muhammad Hisham Kabbani, chairman of the Islamic Supreme Council of America, said, "We would like to advise our government, our congressmen, that there is something big going on and people do not understand it. You have many mosques around the United States...The extremist ideology makes them very active. We can say that they took over 80 per cent of the mosques in the United States." The Mapping Sharia Project confirmed this. They trained former counterintelligence and counterterrorism agents from the FBI, CIA and military — people fluent in Urdu and Arabic — they trained these agents to conduct undercover investigations at American mosques and Islamic centers. They discovered that the *majority* of mosques in the United States (75-80%) are calling for jihad against America, preaching the inferiority of women, promoting hatred of non-Muslims, and selling books, CDs and DVDs encouraging jihad and martyrdom.

Saudi money is building mosques and madrassas all over the world that do the same thing. If you've been wondering why Islamic fundamentalism is expanding so quickly and spreading so widely, now you know.

In other words, this money — what used to be *our* money — is being used to produce well-funded fanatical enemies of America. About ninety percent of *all* Islamic institutions in the *world* are funded by Wahhabis. Saudi Arabia has fewer than two percent of the Muslim population in the world, but they exert a disproportionate influence because of their immense wealth and fanatical zeal. If you recall how fast our oil bill is rising, you can see that it correlates with the rise of jihad worldwide. That immense wealth is having a deleterious impact on world events.

Saudi oil money also finds its way to our universities. Oil-rich princes donate enormous sums for the creation of new "Middle East Studies" departments on college campuses, and for new buildings. A prince will donate 20 million dollars, for example, as Alwaleed bin Talal did for Georgetown University in 2005, and this donation gives him privileges and influence. He gave another $20 million to Harvard.

Go to the link below to see all the American colleges that have received "generous donations" from Saudi oil billionaires.

http://old.nationalreview.com/kurtz/allforeigngiftsreport.html

Big donors are allowed to sit on boards and have a say about what is taught and how it is taught in these departments. Through their Middle East Studies departments, these wealthy Saudi billionaires are helping to promote their agenda on American campuses.

And in what may be an even more insidious trend in the long run, the Saudi government is purchasing controlling interests in American businesses.

Sovereign Wealth Funds

A sovereign wealth fund is an investment fund owned by a *country* rather than owned by a person or business. Sovereign wealth funds invest globally and are composed of financial assets such as stocks, bonds, property, precious metals, etc.

Several Islamic countries have these state-owned investment funds, including Saudi Arabia, and they have inexhaustible wealth at their disposal. They are using it to buy up America (and during recessions, at bargain-basement prices). Their partial ownership of large corporations can often give them a seat on the boards of these companies, which gives them influence in the companies.

They have been particularly intent on investing in media companies in order to influence what Americans believe. In 2007, officials from the 57 countries of the OIC (Organization of Islamic Cooperation) were gathered together for a meeting in Saudi Arabia where they were urged to buy shares in Western media outlets to gain influence over what is communicated to Westerners and *how* it's communicated.

This influence is tangible. The 26th richest man in the world is Alwaleed bin Talal, the Saudi oil billionaire I mentioned above (donating to American colleges). He's the Saudi prince who became famous for offering ten million dollars to then-Mayor Rudy Giuliani (who refused his gift because Talal had blamed 9/11 on American foreign policy).

Talal bought up shares in Fox News until he owned 5.46 percent of Fox's parent company (News Corp.). Even this small percentage gives him influence. He bragged about calling up Rupert Murdoch (News Corp's chairman) a few years ago to complain about the way Fox News was covering the riots in France. Within a half hour of this phone call, Fox News stopped calling them "Muslim riots" and started calling them "civil riots."

Saudi oil billionaires have bought huge blocks of shares of AOL-Time Warner also — the largest media merger in history and still one of the top three largest media companies in the world.

Should We Worry?

Some people find comfort in the belief that we don't have to worry about any of this because the world is going to run out of oil. But Saudi Arabia's oil alone — the *proven* oil still in the ground — is worth $27 trillion. That's worth more than every company traded on the London Stock Exchange *combined*. In fact, it is worth seven *times* all the companies traded on the London Stock Exchange combined.

And what about gas reserves and yet undiscovered oil reserves, in not only Saudi Arabia, but the rest of the OPEC nations? That adds up to an estimated *54 trillion* dollars. And if OPEC keeps raising oil prices, as they have done over the last ten years, it will be worth even more.

So yes, the world will probably eventually run out of oil. But between now and then, OPEC will have gained a terrifying amount of money. They will have bled the world.

As I'm writing this, oil has been hovering at about $100 per barrel. At that rate, OPEC could buy General Motors with six days worth of income. It could buy Apple Computers in two weeks. It could buy the Bank of America with a mere two months of its income.

Most companies require an ownership share of 20% to have a voting block. If OPEC started buying shares in all the S&P 500 companies, it could own 20% of *all* of them within three years.

For these and many other reasons (which include Iran's nuclear program, Venezuela's intolerable human rights abuses, damage to our health and the environment from burning petroleum fuels, etc.) we must stop our own victimization by oil's monopoly. It is dangerous to our national security to send so much money to OPEC nations (Iran, Saudi Arabia, and Venezuela are members of OPEC).

We need to replace oil's destructive monopoly with robust fuel competition and stop relying on a single liquid fuel source for transportation, but create a condition where fuels freely compete with each other. This competition will strip oil of its strategic status, restrain OPEC's income, and reduce the political importance of the unstable Middle East.

This can be done quickly and easily because normal internal combustion engines, like the ones we are driving already, are perfectly capable of burning ethanol, methanol, butanol, propanol, and many other fuels in addition to gasoline — often without any alteration of the car whatsoever.

Oily Industrial Complex

OPEC's monopoly and immense cash flow are not the only dangerous consequences of being stuck in a one-fuel economy. "American" oil companies also benefit from OPEC's policy of keeping prices high. They reap enormous profits year after year, and use the money to hire PR firms and lobbyists, to pay for advertisements which give them influence over what is printed and shown to the public and also provides them with the money to contribute to candidates' political campaigns, which gives them another kind of influence.

Former Representative Herseth Sandlin, an ardent advocate of renewable fuels, said in 2007, "Unfortunately, for the last six years, we've been fighting a tough battle against big oil companies, who have fought us tooth and nail in our efforts to develop a vibrant, sustainable ethanol industry...Red Cavaney, President and CEO of the American Petroleum Institute derided Congressional efforts to promote biofuels like ethanol, calling such efforts 'a joke that is being played on the American people.'"

Even though OPEC controls the world price of oil, *all* oil companies in the world benefit from it. And regardless of the fact that OPEC sets the price far higher than is reasonable for even a very healthy profit, not one oil-producing company in the world sells its oil below the going rate.

In a normal business — where the product does not have a monopoly and where there is no artificially-created scarcity and price-fixing — competing companies sell their product for as low as possible in order to sell more of *their* product than their competitors sell. But because OPEC limits production to keep oil scarce (and therefore expensive), *all* oil available is sold quickly for top dollar. Oil companies don't have to worry that they won't be able to sell their product, so they do not even *try* to compete with each other on price. They take what they can get, producing obscene profits and having plenty of money to pay for propaganda campaigns against anyone who tries to stop them or compete with them.

Oil profits have been used to execute an effective propaganda campaign against oil's most immediately-viable competitor, ethanol.

Alcohol Advocate Silenced

David Blume, author of the book, *Alcohol Can Be a Gas*, and an enthusiastic promoter of alcohol fuel, was asked by San Francisco's PBS station to make a ten-part series entitled, "Alcohol as Fuel" in the early 1980's. Blume had been teaching people how to make their own fuel (ethanol) inexpensively. The PBS series would have made this knowledge available to a much larger audience.

Blume and PBS spent two years filming the series. After the first three segments aired on the San Fransisco PBS station, thousands of people called to order the book Blume had written to accompany the series. But immediately after showing the fourth segment, PBS abruptly canceled the book, which was already at the printer, and canceled the series.

And 120 other PBS stations across the country had already agreed to run the series, but the San Francisco branch suddenly and surprisingly canceled the distribution of the series. It was not shown again anywhere.

What could have caused PBS's sudden change of heart? Especially after seeing the series' obvious popularity?

Blume discovered later that Chevron, a generous donor to PBS, threatened to pull their support unless PBS canceled the series.

In this and many other ways, the oil industry prevents a widespread awareness of its primary rival fuel (alcohol) and actively campaigns against it as it has done since the early 1900s when petroleum organizations first mounted a propaganda campaign against the growing alcohol fuel industry.

Oil companies are still at it today. They give grants to universities and fund studies that show food prices are influenced by the ethanol industry or how alcohol will lower fuel efficiency in cars, etc.; they pay teams of lobbyists and public relations people to keep up a stream of propaganda against ethanol or any alternative fuels. They donate money (to PBS, for example) which gives them the ability to influence programming. They buy advertising in print media and television, which also gives them the power to influence what the public learns. And so on.

Here are a few of the misleading ideas the oil industry has successfully sold to the public:

1. If we use corn for fuel, people will starve, food prices will go up, and Amazon rainforests will be bulldozed.

2. It takes more energy to produce ethanol than you get out of it.

3. There isn't enough farmland to make enough ethanol to replace petroleum.

4. It is bad for the environment to grow crops for fuel.

5. Alcohol fuel is bad for car engines.

All of these statements oversimplify or misrepresent the issue and their insertion into the national conversation has effectively turned many people against an industry that could bring us true energy independence, greatly increase our national security, boost the American economy, produce millions of American jobs, and all while benefiting the environment. It takes a lot of money to accomplish such a thing. But they have got money to burn.

The misleading ideas on the list above help maintain oil's monopoly over transportation fuel — they impede the achievement of our greatest hope for salvation — fuel competition.

These ideas have not only made their way into the national conscience, they have been directly inserted into the ears of politicians. Oil money is influencing what the media will air, what American schools will teach, and how our own government is run.

Saudi Influence on the U.S. Government

Saudi oil billionaires have hired American law firms and lobbying organizations to promote their agenda within the U.S. political system. They keep these powerful groups on their full-time payroll. The Saudis alone have 100 lobbyists in Washington (the NRA, considered one of the most powerful lobbies in Washington D.C., has 28 lobbyists). According to OpenSecrets.org, the total number of lobbyists reported for the year 2012 who were working for the oil and gas industry is 736! But let's just focus on the Saudis for now.

They not only have 100 lobbyists who spend their time persuading our politicians to adopt their point of view, but the Saudis influence individual politicians directly through the incentive of money, and it's all perfectly legal.

In chapter three of Robert Zubrin's book, *Energy Victory*, he details the amazing system of Saudi oil-money payoffs to American politicians. I'll give you a few highlights here.

Many of the ways money directly influences politicians are officially declared as such. But there are "innumerable other influentials who accept well-paid consultancies from the Saudis and who chose not to make the connection public," wrote Zubrin. "One of these appears to be former secretary of state Henry Kissinger, who had to resign from his position as head of the September 11 investigative commission when he was asked to disclose his client list."

He wasn't the only one. Senator George Mitchell, former Senate majority leader, had to quit his position as vice chair for the same reason.

Another way Saudis influence American politicians is by spending big money for weapons made by American companies. The Saudis have spent about *100 billion dollars* on sophisticated weapons they have not used (because Saudi Arabia is protected by the United States military). Their purchases give them influence — what the defense contractors' say to politicians can be manipulated by the Saudis.

And since big defense contracts create lots of jobs, the Saudi influence spreads to the politicians in whose districts those jobs will be created.

Another way to legally give money to influential American politicians is through making a politician a board member of a corporation, and generously paying them for their "service."

Here's how it works: Saudi funds are used to create a business partnership. An important political figure is then invited to sit on the board. The business then pays the politician a fantastic sum for basically doing nothing. For example, according to the *New York Times*, former secretary of state James Baker has received *180 million dollars* for his board membership in the Carlyle Group, an investment firm funded largely by Saudis.

This is not an isolated case. Far from it. According to former CIA counterterrorism case officer Robert Baer, author of *Sleeping With the Devil*, "...almost every Washington figure worth mentioning has served on the board of at least one company that did a deal with Saudi Arabia."

Another legal way money is transferred to politicians is to invite influential people onto the board of a corporation and give them stock options in the company. The politician serves on the board for short time, and then cashes out the stock options, often reaping huge profits.

Many people, justifiably alarmed at our situation — the price of fuel, its effect on the economy, the oil industry's fuel monopoly, and the influence of oil money on U.S. politics — want to do something to stop it. We desperately need "energy independence" (specifically, *fuel* independence). The two biggest and most obvious solutions have been to *drill more* of our own oil, or *use less* oil (lower the speed limit, produce smaller cars with better fuel efficiency, encourage more public transportation, etc.)

Drill more or use less. These both seem like reasonable methods to reduce our dependence on foreign oil, but neither has a hope of solving the problem. Let's look at them separately and find out why.

Drilling More

It seems obvious that if American oil companies drilled more oil in America, Saudi Arabia would get less of our money and gasoline prices for Americans would come down.

But that isn't the case.

The fundamental problem with the assumption that "drilling more will help" is that *American oil companies are not "ours."* They are not owned by the government. They have no legal obligation to represent the interests of the American people. So they charge American consumers the same price they would charge anyone else in the world, and the world oil price is set by OPEC.

So no matter how much oil "we" drill in America, what drivers pay at American gas stations remains unaffected.

Although it's true that if we drilled more oil in America and if it was sold exclusively to Americans, OPEC would not make any money from Americans (except where OPEC nations have invested in American oil companies), OPEC nations would still sell all the oil they wanted to pump to everyone else in the world, still reap unbelievable windfalls week after week, and still have money to influence our government. Saudi Arabia would still have plenty of money to spread Wahhabism, OPEC would still control the price of oil so gasoline at American pumps wouldn't be any cheaper, and the American economy would still be vulnerable to the hostile whims of OPEC nations because their production affects the rest of the world (and the global economy affects *our* economy).

Oil's worldwide monopoly on transportation fuel would remain unchanged.

Drilling "our own" oil *would* improve America's trade deficit, and it *would* generate American jobs. But if it doesn't lower gas prices, if it keeps us stuck as a one-fuel economy, if it keeps our economy stuck riding the ups and downs of OPEC's whims, and if it keeps the money flowing to OPEC from the rest of the world, drilling more is only a partial solution at best.

Another factor to consider is that the easy oil in America is gone. The oil still to be extracted is more difficult to recover and as time goes on, will be ever more expensive to drill and ever more damaging to the environment.

But what if America found huge, as-yet-undiscovered easy-to-recover oil deposits and drilled so much oil that it flooded the whole world with oil? Wouldn't *that* lower world oil prices?

Unfortunately, no. Quite a few large oil discoveries have been made since the advent of OPEC, and those new sources have dramatically raised the amount of oil on the world market. In fact, total world oil production has *doubled* since the creation of OPEC.

OPEC has responded to every new abundance of oil on the world market by lowering its production to maintain sufficient oil scarcity to keep the price where they want it. And, of course, world demand keeps rising — a factor that helps OPEC keep oil scarce.

What happens if America finds such an abundance of oil they are able to produce as much as Saudi Arabia? Wouldn't that solve the problem? No, unfortunately. America would have to form a coalition with other oil producing states that was big enough that their combined production could set the world price for oil, but since that is against American law, it would not happen. One country alone would not be able to do it, even with as much oil as Saudi Arabia, who joined with eleven other countries to form OPEC because they couldn't do it alone.

Besides that, American oil producers might be in the same position as American farmers when they grew so much grain they dropped the price low enough to to make farming unprofitable. The new oil finds in America are not easy to get to. They require new and expensive technologies. The only reason these methods are being pursued is because OPEC is keeping oil prices high, so those investments are justifiable. If oil prices dropped worldwide, those oil extraction methods may very well become unprofitable.

To understand clearly how the cartel is able to alter the world price of oil, imagine a giant tub full of oil. This represents the world's oil supply at the moment. A spigot at the bottom of the pool is draining oil out at a steady rate. This represents the world's use of its present oil supply. Over time, it drains out at a faster pace (the world's use of oil is rising), but it is pretty steady. At the top of this tub are many spigots *adding* oil. These represent all the different sources of oil in the world — the oil rigs off the coast of southern California, the wells in Saudi Arabia and Norway, oil fields in Texas and Canada, etc. Each of them are pouring oil into the tub at a fairly steady rate.

If you add *extra* oil — if a major new oil field is discovered, for example, the rate at which the tub fills would be faster than the rate the tub empties, so the level of the oil in the tub would begin to rise. Oil would be more abundant in the world, so the price per barrel would drop. But OPEC prevents this from happening. They restrict their 12 large spigots (which totals 42% of the world's production) to keep the level steady, keeping the world's supply of oil at any given moment the same, which keeps the price the same (or rising).

This tactic by OPEC also conserves their oil reserves. Everyone else in the world is extracting oil as fast as they can, using up their smaller reserves at a faster rate than the OPEC nations, so you think they have us over a barrel now? Wait until the rest of the world runs out!

In 2011, in the midst of a recession, with people driving much less, and with more fuel efficient cars on the road (in other words, Americans were buying less gasoline), the second-largest American oil company, Chevron, had "a 43 percent jump in quarterly profit," according to a *New York Times* article.

"The numbers released on Friday were the latest in a string of huge profits from the industry, which got a lift from the highest oil prices in nearly three years... Chevron's profit rose to $7.7 billion...from $5.4 billion ...a year earlier."

In other words, this *American* oil company is benefiting greatly from OPEC's desire to gouge the world. The oil Chevron pumps from American oil fields is sold to Americans at *OPEC's* price, generating indecent profits at a time Americans are suffering financially. They are not selling their oil at "competitive prices" as they could easily do and still make a healthy profit. They're selling it at OPEC's prices, which are so high above the American company's costs for production, their profits runneth over. And they are not alone.

The Huffington Post wrote, "The sputtering economy, high unemployment rate and punishing gas prices are taking a huge toll on average Americans, but at least somebody is doing well: The Big Five oil companies this week announced they had made a whopping $36 billion in profits in the second quarter of 2011." ExxonMobil had profits 41 percent higher than the same period of the previous year and 161 percent higher than the year before.

But back to the question here: Will drilling more American oil bring us "energy independence?" Will it break oil's monopoly? Will it at least lower gas prices? The Associated Press (AP) did a statistical analysis of 36 years of gas prices to see if prices correlated with domestic oil production. They don't correlate at all, of course, as counterintuitive as that seems to someone who doesn't know how it works.

How much oil the U.S. drills has *nothing* to do with the price we pay at the pump. In the last few years, domestic oil production has gone up significantly, but in that time, the price at the pump has skyrocketed. "It was a case of drilling more and paying much more," wrote the authors of the AP analysis.

Drilling more American oil will not and cannot lower gasoline prices.

This is not to say it will be any cheaper to buy it anywhere else. Yes, as long as we are using oil, we should drill it in America. It will at least improve the trade deficit and create American jobs. But if we want to pay less at the pump and free ourselves from oil's virtual monopoly, gasoline needs competition. Drilling more will not provide that.

Using Less Oil

Another possible solution to our "overdependence on foreign oil" is *conservation*. Several strong attempts have been made to encourage conservation nationwide, with some success.

But America's overall oil consumption has risen anyway (population is increasing, so more cars are on the road). The *world* consumption of oil has also risen dramatically as millions of Chinese and Indians have begun buying cars. OPEC still controls the price of oil and thus our economy, and still rakes in huge profits for their hostile regimes. Conserving is powerless to change any of this.

But when people use less oil, it should theoretically make oil more abundant on the world market, right? This should lower world oil prices. But it doesn't. OPEC consistently responds to conservation efforts by lowering their production, making oil scarcer, and raising the price up to what OPEC wants.

Trying to reduce waste is a good idea anyway. It helps lower pollution, and saves money. Why burn two gallons of fuel to get somewhere when you can do it with one, if the technology exists to make that possible?

But it doesn't solve the other problems, and they are too important to dismiss.

In the long run, conservation *alone* only prolongs and perpetuates oil's monopoly of transportation fuel.

The Joy of Gouging

Unlike other commodities (that *compete* in the marketplace) the world price OPEC sets for oil has no relation to what it costs to produce the oil. Oil companies could make a handsome profit at 20 or 30 dollars a barrel. In 1999, Saudi Oil Minister Ali al-Naimi publicly admitted that the all-inclusive cost of producing a barrel of oil in Saudi Arabia — which has the easiest-to-produce oil in the world — is $1.50. That is not a typo. A buck fifty. Right now the world price is over $100 a barrel, and the country that has the most influence on that price is Saudi Arabia.

Worldwide, it costs most oil producers about $5 to produce a barrel of oil.

The oil industry is shamelessly *gouging*. Regardless of the worldwide recession, and regardless of the fact that any one of them could easily undercut their "competitors" and still make huge profits, not one of them does it. They charge whatever they can get because they will quickly sell all they can produce.

OPEC has us over a barrel. They know it and we know it.

So here we are: Dictators and princes are illegally swindling and essentially robbing billions of people, and using that money to make the world a more dangerous, unstable, misogynistic, repressive place. And the country who buys the most oil is the United States. You and me.

How We Got Stuck on the Petroleum Standard

People often talk about "energy independence" without making the distinction between electricity and fuel. America is already energy independent with electricity. Only one percent of electricity in America is generated by oil. We produce our electricity domestically.

What we *don't* have is *fuel* independence. Our vehicles burn petroleum. When you go to the pump, in all but a very few stations, your choice is petroleum or petroleum. It's a monopoly, and that's the problem.

But there was a time when America was fuel independent because we had fuel competition. In fact, *gasoline* was the alternative fuel. Alcohol was the primary fuel because it was more widely available, has much higher octane, and burns cleaner than gasoline.

The first successful modern-style combustion engines produced by Nikolaus August Otto used alcohol for fuel. In the 1890s trains, farm machinery and cars used alcohol for fuel in Europe and the United States.

The extremely successful Model T was a flex fuel vehicle — made to run on either alcohol or gasoline, or both. Gas stations were becoming abundant in cities, but out in the countryside they were few and far between.

Most farms had alcohol stills, however. Farmers used stills to turn their crop waste and surplus grain into a storable valuable product: Alcohol. They used alcohol for heating, light, and power (most farmers did not have electricity in the 1800s and early 1900s).

Alcohol is also compact and easy to transport. Surplus grain and fruit is bulky, it can rot, it can be eaten by pests, and isn't worth very much at the marketplace anyway. Alcohol has none of those disadvantages.

Because most farms had alcohol available, if you were driving your Model T out in the countryside and were running low on fuel, you could stop at almost any farm and refuel with alcohol, no problem.

If you were a farmer yourself, you could fill your tank with your own homemade fuel.

This is why it was so practical to make the Model T a flex fuel vehicle. The car was built with a lever on the steering column, allowing the driver to adjust the timing, and a knob next to the steering wheel to adjust the carburetor. Alcohol and gasoline have different requirements, and once the car was started, the driver could easily adjust the car manually until the car was running nicely (doing it "by ear") no matter what mixture was in the fuel tank.

The Model T, then, was a platform upon which fuels could compete.

The First Oil Monopoly

As the affordable and reliable Model T cars were flying off the assembly line at breakneck speed, Standard Oil, run by John D. Rockefeller, was busy crushing its competition, buying up smaller oil businesses and fuel stations, until he owned a monopoly on gasoline in America.

There was only one competitor left: Alcohol.

Because the competition wasn't centrally located in large facilities or companies — because it was so widespread and small scale — Rockefeller couldn't put all the farmers with their stills out of business with his usual tactics of intimidation, buying them out, or undercutting their prices to drive them into bankruptcy.

But he did something that, seen in retrospect, was an amazingly creative and devastatingly effective strategy. Whether he did it deliberately to crush his alcohol competition or not (he never said), it certainly did cripple Standard Oil's last rival.

Rockefeller gave a huge sum of money to the Anti-Saloon League, whose mission was to illegalize the drinking of alcohol beverages.

The Anti-Saloon League was not interested in temperance, as other anti-alcohol movements were. They aimed for nothing less than total *prohibition*. With Rockefeller's money, they ramped up their campaign, and with Rockefeller's influence on American politicians, something that now seems impossible was achieved — not just a bill, but an *amendment to the Constitution* banning the making, selling, and transporting of liquor, instantly illegalizing the farmers' stills all over the country and wiping out the last threat to oil's total dominance of the fuel market.

That was in 1920. Prohibition lasted until 1933 — long enough to cause automakers to stop making flex fuel cars. Ford stopped in 1931.

Petroleum had won. It achieved a monopoly over the transportation fuel market that has continued to this day.

But the petroleum monopoly and its control over the world's economy reached a whole new level of menace the day OPEC came into existence.

The Creation of OPEC

Iran, Iraq, Saudi Arabia, Kuwait, and Venezuela got together and founded OPEC in 1960. They had seen that a small disruption in the supply of oil could raise the world price dramatically. They discovered this by accident. A bulldozer in Libya accidentally backed into a pipeline and shut it down, which temporarily made about three percent of the world's oil supply unavailable. People began bidding for what was left, and the world price of oil skyrocketed.

The original OPEC nations figured that the five of them together had control of a large enough percentage of the world's oil production that if they agreed on production quotas, they could set whatever price they wanted.

The first time they exercised their power was in 1973. The United States backed Israel in the Yom Kippur war. OPEC nations didn't like this, so they retaliated with an oil embargo that caused gas shortages and sent America (and the rest of the world) into a steep recession.

And OPEC has raised and lowered its production quotas ever since, sending the world into recessions again and again. Whenever oil prices rise high enough, a recession is inevitable. Ten of the eleven recessions since WWII were brought on by a rise in oil prices.

Every president since Richard Nixon, (the president during the first oil embargo) has declared his commitment to make America "energy independent." During his presidency, Nixon boldly declared, "Let us set as our national goal, in the spirit of Apollo, with the determination of the Manhattan Project, that by the end of this decade we will have developed the potential to meet our own energy needs without depending on any foreign energy source."

President Gerald Ford said, "I am recommending a plan to make us invulnerable to cutoffs of foreign oil…"

President Jimmy Carter said our need to become independent of foreign oil was the "moral equivalent of war." After the first oil embargo, and then the 1979 oil crisis, it was clear something needed to be done. During the Carter administration, many new programs were created, and it began a boom in the construction of ethanol plants.

Ronald Reagan said we should rely on "native American genius, not arbitrary federal policy, to be free to provide for our energy future."

Prior to the first Gulf War in 1991, President George H.W. Bush said, "There is no security for the United States in further dependence on foreign oil."

In 2000, President Clinton said, "The nation's growing reliance on imports threatens the nation's security because it increases U.S. vulnerability to oil supply interruptions."

George W. Bush insisted in his 2003 State of the Union address that one of the goals of his administration was "to promote energy independence for our country."

Barack Obama said: "America's dependence on oil is one of the most serious threats that our nation has faced."

All these earnest statements by the most powerful leaders of the free world combined with the fact that we still rely completely on oil, makes the goal seem futile. But we haven't failed utterly. Far from it. We've successfully attained energy independence with *electricity* production.

The question we should be asking is, "How did we do it?"

We were able to accomplish it by having *multiple sources*. We use coal, nuclear power, natural gas, hydroelectric, wind, solar, geothermal, and biomass to generate electricity in the United States, and we use almost no oil (it's too expensive so it can't compete).

We are using an ever-growing variety of sources — and they are all sources available within our own country. *That* is the key to energy independence.

We've done it with electricity. We can do it with fuel.

We could successfully fulfill the commitments of the last eight presidents. It will require something beyond drilling more oil and using less. A game-changing project in the 1980s demonstrated how it might be done.

The Invention That Changed The World

Roberta J. Nichols was an extraordinary and distinguished engineer, specializing in internal combustion engines. In the 1970s she was the leading researcher at Ford for "alternative fuel vehicles." Nichols was in the right place at the right time, and she was the perfect person for the job.

The timing could not possibly have been better. With the oil embargo in 1973 and the Iranian revolution, American leaders were perfectly clear that we needed an alternative fuel — and it had to be something we had more control over than oil. Air pollution was becoming an important policy issue too, so people were looking at methanol as an alternative fuel. It can be produced domestically and economically, and it creates significantly fewer emissions than gasoline.

Methanol was the perfect answer.

Nichols had grown up in Los Angeles and knew some of the right people, so she was able to convince the state of California to launch a program to test the practicality of methanol as a fuel. Then she convinced Ford to invest in it.

In 1980, Ford bequeathed to the Californian government twelve Pintos that had been altered to run on methanol. Within three years, California had a fleet of over six hundred methanol cars.

The cars were a great success in many ways. The drivers loved them. Methanol is 105 octane, significantly increasing the effective horsepower of the state cars.

After these methanol cars were driven a total of about 35 million miles, Nichols and her team had lots of data. The emissions were low, the fuel-efficiency was good, and everything seemed wonderful.

But there was a problem. California only had 22 methanol fueling stations in the whole state. Because the cars they were using were simply retrofitted gasoline cars, the gas tanks weren't big enough (methanol is not very dense, so uses more liquid per mile). They had a 230-mile range, but with so few methanol stations, that was sometimes not good enough.

Because there were only about 600 methanol-burning cars in the whole state of California, gas stations owners didn't have much incentive to add methanol pumps. So the drivers had to constantly worry about running out of fuel.

And of course, nobody else wanted to buy a methanol car because of the shortage of fuel stations. So California was in the same Catch-22 we find ourselves

in today — the fueling stations want to wait until there
are enough cars on the road that are capable of burning alcohol before they add a pump for it, and car buy-
ers are reluctant to buy a car that burns a fuel hardly
anybody sells.

At the time, Nichols and her team were not overly
bothered by this. They originally wanted to test the
technical feasibility of methanol-burning cars, and all
the tests came out great, so their *experiment* was a success.

The *car*, however, was a failure — but only because of the lack of infrastructure to support it.

Nichols still loved the idea of methanol cars, and
she kept thinking about it. She realized that if her
methanol car was ever going to be widely accepted, the
car *itself* would have to solve the problem. They could
not rely on preexisting infrastructure (fuel stations) to
bridge the gap. That meant the car would have to be
capable of burning *both* methanol and gasoline, so
when drivers couldn't find a methanol station, they
could get by with gasoline.

Creating a methanol-only car was not that difficult
from an engineering standpoint. But a mixed-fuel car
was something else. It would be easy if the car always
had the *same* mixture of fuels, whatever that mixture
was, as long as it was always consistent. But to create
an engine that could effectively deal with a mixture of
changing proportions was a challenge.

But if a methanol car was ever going to enter the
mainstream, that's what they needed to do. The car
would somehow have to be designed to respond to
whatever arbitrary mixture of fuels it was burning at

40

the moment, and to change in response to changing mixtures. At the time, this was unheard of, and they didn't know how to go about it.

The Model T used manual controls, adjusted by ear. Modern cars were too quiet and used fuel injectors. This was a new technical problem.

Their solution was to adapt an invention by G.A. Schwippert — a sensor that could determine the alcohol content of a liquid using light refraction, and then it fed that changing information to the fuel injector.

With the sensor in place, the fuel-to-air ratio was automatically changed on the spot, depending on the fuel mixture of the moment. It was brilliant and simple. And it worked.

Nichols and her team invented the first modern flex fuel vehicle.

Ford Motor Company made quite a few of these methanol-gasoline cars, and other automakers experimented with them too, but they didn't catch on as quickly as Nichols had hoped, partly because in the mid-1980s world oil prices dropped so low that methanol was no longer cost-competitive. Did OPEC deliberately drop oil prices to kill off the many budding alternative fuel programs popping up all over the world? That's one of the primary techniques most monopolies have traditionally used to eliminate competition. In our view, it seems likely.

But regardless of what happened to methanol, the farm lobby, which was looking for a market for their surplus corn, helped keep the flex fuel vehicle idea alive. They helped promote ethanol and flex fuel cars, and that is why today flex fuel cars are warranted to burn gasoline and ethanol, but not methanol. There were no powerful lobbyists pushing to warrant cars to burn methanol in their flex fuel vehicles. Methanol had no champions in Congress, so today we see no methanol pumps anywhere and we have no cars on the road warranted to burn it.

Roberta J. Nichols died in 2005. But she left behind a legacy that will change the world. The technology to make flex fuel cars has continued to evolve and improve. With already-existing technology it is easily possible (although not yet legal) to make a car that can burn gasoline, ethanol, methanol, and butanol in any proportion or combination, making that car capable of a level of fuel competition that has never been known before.

How well we take advantage of our new capabilities will largely depend on what we think we know.

Revisiting What "Everybody Knows"

People "know" all kinds of mistaken notions about alcohol fuel — it ruins car engines, causes food shortages, uses more energy to create than it produces, and so on. How did these ideas arrive in so many minds with so much credibility?

The answer is simple: We have been the victims of an effective propaganda campaign. We've been paying an unnecessarily high price for gasoline, and the oil industry has been reaping excessive profit for decades. With so much money at its disposal, the petroleum industry spends lavishly on public relations projects. "One prong in the oil industry's strategy," wrote David Kiley for *Bloomberg Businessweek*, "is an anti-ethanol information campaign." It would be more accurate to call it a disinformation campaign.

The result: Politicians and ordinary citizens have a strong bias against clean-burning, American-made, re-newable, economy-lifting, national-security-boosting alcohol fuels. Here's a fuel that has the potential to save us in many different ways, and yet there is suspicion, indifference, or outright animosity toward alcohol fuel in the minds of many people.

And the oil industry has done more than try to discredit alcohol fuel. They've actively blocked our access to it. We have 160,000 stations today with gasoline pumps and only 2,900 stations with at least one E85 pump (85% ethanol, 15% gasoline), and not one station selling M85 (85% methanol, 15% gasoline).

Most of the 2,900 E85 pumps are at independent stations because oil companies have tried to block E85 being sold at their stations. They've used several tactics according to a report by the Consumer Federation of America. One is a requirement that the franchise owners must buy all their fuel from the oil company. Another is requiring franchise owners to sign a contract that limits how much they can advertise E85. Some contracts dictate that if a station owner puts in an E85 pump, it must be on a separate island and not under the main canopy. Loren Beard, senior manager for energy planning and policy for Chrysler put it succinctly: "Big Oil is at the top of the list for blocking the spread of ethanol acceptance by consumers and the marketplace."

So our access to alcohol fuel has been restricted, and we've been on the receiving end of some serious spin. And we have paid dearly for it. The lack of competition bleeds our economy of its wealth.

One of the most common criticisms of the ethanol industry is that growing all that corn and converting it into fuel raises the cost of food. It is known as the "food versus fuel debate." Seems pretty straightforward, doesn't it? I mean, on a common-sense level, it would seem obvious that if you take part of your food and make fuel out of it, then it would make food scarcer and thus raise the price of the food you have left, right? But sometimes reality is counterintuitive. Studies show that making ethanol from corn has almost no impact on food prices, and may even help *prevent* rising food prices, *and* it has definitely lowered the price of gasoline at the pump (because ethanol is added to gasoline).

And yet when the food versus fuel debate is mentioned, it is usually not even stated outright, but is stated as a forgone conclusion — because "everyone knows" already that making fuel from corn causes a shortage of food.

I just watched a video of Representative Herseth Sandlin questioning oil executives from five different oil companies at a hearing. At one point, one of the executives, Peter Robinson, Vice Chairman of Chevron, said, "I do believe that going over ten percent in the nation (blending more than ten percent ethanol into regular gasoline) would stretch the food system to the point where you don't want to go any further."

Rep. Sandlin knew ethanol doesn't create food shortages or raise prices significantly, so she challenged this. She asked if *any* of these oil executive knew of *any* analysis they could cite showing that ethanol raises food prices.

All of them said no.

In May, 2013, the World Bank (a group of five large, influential, and closely associated organizations that work collaboratively to reduce poverty in developing countries) published a study showing clearly and unequivocally that *high crude oil prices* are the most significant cause high food prices.

The authors of the study looked at five different internationally traded food commodities (corn, wheat, rice, soybean and palm oil). As public policy analyst Gal Sitty writes, they sought "to determine the impact of oil prices, exchange rates, interest rates, stock-to-use ratio, GDP and the price of manufacturing exports on each of the five food commodities. This method led the World Bank researchers to conclude that for all of commodities studied, corn included, oil prices had the biggest impact. In fact, the analysis showed that oil prices were significantly more influential than the next-most influential factor, the stocks-to-use factor (a ratio of the available food stocks compared to consumption), and were even found to account for a full two-thirds of the rise of the price of wheat."

It's brilliant, really (although criminal) to deflect the blame for what their own industry is causing while simultaneously discrediting their biggest competitor.

What You May Not Have Noticed

Have you ever wondered why you've never heard a "food versus *flowers* debate?" After all, we have an enormous amount of farmland devoted to raising flowers. I've stood in places where as far as you can see in every direction are endless fields of flowers growing on prime farmland.

How many giant greenhouses are used to grow flowers in the United States?

Shouldn't all these resources be used for *food?* Are all these fields and greenhouses causing worldwide starvation? Is the massive flower industry raising the price of food? Certainly if all those fields were used for growing food crops, the price of food would drop.

But we don't hear anything about a "food versus flowers" debate. Are flowers more important than food? Are flowers more important than fuel? No, and that's not the issue anyway. The source of the "food versus fuel" debate is fuel alcohol's most dangerous competitor — the oil industry. Those who have the most to lose from the rising popularity of alcohol fuels created the "debate" and introduced it into the public dialog.

The petroleum industry coined the phrase (food versus fuel) in 1979 and then they teamed up with the packaged food industry to try to destroy ethanol in 2008. And because the alcohol fuel industry is (at the moment anyway) dwarfed by the immense wealth of the oil industry, the myth-busting facts haven't reached nearly the number of people who have heard the food versus fuel idea, and millions of people have bought the phony "debate" hook, line, and sinker.

The flower industry is only one of many we could mention. How about booze? How much land is devoted to raising crops just for liquor or beer? Shouldn't that land be devoted to *food?* How many calories worth of potential food crops does it take to make a bottle of bourbon or a case of beer? Why don't we hear of a "food versus booze" debate? Or is booze more important than transportation? It seems to me I *need* to get to work, but I don't *need* to get a buzz (or buy flowers, for that matter).

What about Christmas trees? What about dog and cat food? Are these more important than starving people or transportation?

I could go on and on. In fact, I *will* go on and on (in a minute), but you've gotten the main point already. I'm going to beat this issue to death, though, because this mistaken notion is a major impediment to fuel competition. The phony issue shows up in articles and books and interviews, and it is completely taken for granted by most of the people who mention it, even though several impartial researchers have shown that food prices have only risen *slightly* because of the ethanol industry.

And it has also been shown that the largest influence on rising food prices is *rising oil prices*. Oil prices and food prices are directly and necessarily correlated. That, however, is almost never mentioned anywhere.

And the slight impact the ethanol industry has had on corn prices has actually been a *good* thing for the hungry people of the world, for two reasons. First, America's successful production of abundant grain (along with our government's subsidizing its exportation) dropped the price of grain so low that small farmers in developing countries couldn't sell their grain locally at a price high enough to keep them in business.

Jack Wilkinson, former president of the International Federation of Agricultural Producers said, "Up until very, very recently, surplus corn in the United States and Europe got dumped in the African market and actually destroyed the commercial market for those farmers."

Jeff Broin, the founder and CEO of POET, which is the world's largest ethanol producer said, "Because the U.S. and Europe have been subsidizing grain for about fifty years, there's a billion acres of land around the world that has gone out of production. It's gone fallow."

So ethanol's small impact on food prices has been a good thing, encouraging small, local farming operations to spring up around the world, which is increasing the world's food supply. And if we can get half of American drivers to switch to alcohol fuel, those farmers in developing nations may get a chance to do more than merely grow food; they'll have an opportunity to turn their surplus crops into ethanol and export it to a fuel-hungry world, which could help them rise up out of poverty.

But like I said, I intend to beat this issue to death. Are you ready? Besides the food versus flowers debate and the food versus booze debate, what else can we look at? What other good potential croplands are being "wasted" when there are starving people in the world?

How about wine? Why don't we have a food versus wine debate? There are *millions* of acres of wine grapes planted worldwide. One single variety, Airén — an undistinguished white grape — is planted on more than one million acres in central Spain alone. Is wine more important than food?

How many acres are devoted to football fields? Baseball fields? Soccer fields? How about a food versus football debate? A football field, including end zones, is 1.3 acres. Almost every junior high school, high school, and college that plays interscholastic football has their own football field. That would put the number of football fields in America up into the thousands, probably the tens of thousands.

I am not suggesting we get rid of football fields. Not at all. It is completely unnecessary. We have plenty of farmland to grow both food and fuel, and so does the rest of the world. I'm bringing this up to point out that other perfectly legitimate potential cropland targets are never mentioned, because the source of the criticism is the oil industry, and their target is the ethanol industry.

What about lawns? I'm not even talking about the acres devoted to people's front and backyards, although those should count too, since that alone adds up to *thirty million acres* in the United States. But many farmland acres are devoted to growing sod or turf used for planting lawns and golf courses, football fields, baseball fields, soccer fields, etc. In the state of Texas alone, 54,000 acres are devoted to growing sod or turf.

Mowed lawns are the largest crop by weight in the U.S. Is all the land devoted to lawns in the U.S. more important than food or fuel? Why don't we have a food versus lawns debate?

We feed nearly all our millions of acres of corn to cows. It takes seventeen to twenty pounds of grain to produce one pound of beef. Worried about starving poor? Become a vegetarian. Is the deliciousness of beef more important than transportation? Why not stop feeding cows and feed people instead? Please don't accuse me of being a vegetarian. I love meat, and I'm going to keep eating it. But according to the USDA, for the last five years, the amount of corn used for animal feed is roughly equal to the amount used to make ethanol, but we hear almost nothing about the "grain versus meat" debate. Even without becoming a vegetarian, we could eat grass-fed beef to save that grain for starving people, right? And a huge amount of corn is used to make high-fructose corn syrup. Do we really need that much sweetener? Couldn't the corn be used in healthier ways to feed more people?

What about tobacco? Is it more important than food? What about a "food versus coffee" controversy? How much land is devoted to coffee and tea in the world? Are coffee and tea more important than food? More important than fuel?

And the biggest source of untapped food is *waste*. According to experts who study it, like the economist Mancur Olson, an astonishing 30 to 50 percent of all the food produced is never eaten! In poorer countries, most of this waste is from the crops rotting in the fields, being eaten by rats, or spoiling in transit. In richer countries, most of the waste is from excess that is thrown away — salad, bread, fruit, vegetables, etc.

Regardless of what else we do, we definitely need to tackle the food versus waste issue.

According to a study at UC Davis, winemakers create leftover fruit scraps — the mashed up skins and stems — that can be used for ethanol production. In California alone, the winemakers produce more than

100,000 *tons* of grape scrap per year, and most of it is simply thrown away.

But the point of all this is that oil money buys influence, and the oil industry has decided, and I think quite astutely, that one way to cripple the ethanol industry — one way to undermine popular support for their strongest competitor — is to make people believe that growing crops for ethanol will cause people to starve. It's a clever tactic. Let's hope a growing number of people will see through it.

One finding that might help people see through it is the tight correlation of food prices with oil prices. In 2008, for instance, world oil prices shot up to $140 for a barrel of oil. And as it rose, corn prices shot up to $7 a bushel (which is really high). Then in 2009, oil prices dropped to $40 a barrel, and corn dropped to $3 a bushel. If you see it on a graph, you see corn prices track oil prices. And the same is true of other grains and foods. But you do *not* see a correlation between how much ethanol is made into corn and how much a bushel of corn costs.

When corn dropped to $3 a bushel, was it because we were using less ethanol? No. In fact, production had *risen* almost ten percent. Corn prices do not track ethanol output, but they do track oil prices.

The Chinese Want to Eat More Pork

Let's look at this from another angle. As more people in China have more money to spend, one of the things they want to spend it on is pork. So the demand for pork is rising. And with it, the demand for feed is rising. Specifically, the demand for corn. I keep coming across news stories with titles like these:

China's Corn Imports May Top 10 Million Tons
China's Taste for Pork Continues to Grow
China's Hunger for Pork to Boost Corn Demand

To quote from the third article: "Rather than becoming more dependent on imported meat, Mr. Urlich expects China will favour purchasing more feed grains. This should lead to a greater reliance on imported corn for the growing livestock and poultry sector.

"In fact, both the UN's Food and Agriculture Organization and China's state-affiliated agricultural information service provider, estimate that corn imports will reach 5 million tons in 2011/2012 from 1.5 million tons in the previous year."

Those who say we should not use "food" to make fuel may not mean to say it, but what they're unwittingly proposing is something like this: "We should forget about energy independence, national security, and economic vitality so people in China can eat more pork."

In other words, the "food versus fuel" argument means we should not use our land to grow feedstocks to make fuel, but instead we should use it to grow corn and export it to China because they really like pork.

I think if most Americans were given the choice, we would choose to give up our addiction to oil, and leave it to China to work out their pork addiction problem themselves.

I'd like to clarify that. We are *not* addicted to oil. We are the victims of an illegal transportation fuel monopoly. The moment we have access to a better fuel, we will drop oil like a hot rock. The *oil companies* want us to stick with oil, but American drivers would *love* to be free of oil's fuel monopoly and the high prices, high pollution, and high level of terrorist threat it causes.

The Whiskey Rebellion

The famous Whiskey Rebellion occurred in September, 1791. Farmers were rebelling against a tax on their whiskey making — a tax they perceived as unfair and harmful to their livelihood.

Back then, farmers "out West" (western Pennsylvania) had solved a problem in an ingenious way, and they didn't want it taken away from them. The problem was surplus corn. What can a farmer do with surplus corn? They could try to ship it back east to sell it, but it's bulky and expensive to ship. And it can rot, it gets eaten by bugs and mice, etc. Their solution was to turn it into whiskey (ethanol). So most farmers had a still. They transformed their excess corn into whiskey, which was valuable and condensed (easy to ship). It did not go bad. Mice couldn't destroy it.

They turned their surplus corn into something wanted and valuable. It was an elegant solution.

Flash forward to the 20th century. American farmers were continually suffering from massive surpluses which flooded the world market with cheap grain. There was so much surplus, grain prices around the world dropped out the bottom. Many farmers went bankrupt. They couldn't sell their grain for enough money to stay in business. They were *too* successful at increasing their crop yields!

So what did they do? They tried to find other markets for their excess grain. One of the things they came up with was high-fructose corn syrup.

And another market they found was fuel. They began doing what their predecessors were doing back in the Whiskey Rebellion days — they turned their excess grain into ethanol.

But (music changes to a sinister tone) their success began to eat into the gasoline market. Because ethanol burns cleaner and has a higher octane rating, many states mandated it as an additive to gasoline. And as ethanol became more widely known, people wanted to use it more and more. In places like Los Angeles, a higher percentage of alcohol was mandated to be added to gasoline to cut down on pollution (and it greatly reduced the number and severity of their "smog alerts").

So the oil industry went on a propaganda rampage against ethanol, as you've already read about. And when food prices rose sharply in 2008, the oil industry PR people exploited it by implicating the ethanol industry in raising food prices. But as you've already learned, ethanol had almost no influence on the steep rise of food prices. The biggest culprit was oil prices.

The irony is that the ethanol industry was created in the first place because food prices were too *low!*

Pundits were crying out a warning that because of ethanol, food would get too expensive. People in poor countries would starve because of our greedy need for fuel, etc. But in fact, in many ways, just the *opposite* is true. Most of the criticism about food-versus-fuel is centered on corn, so let's look more closely at that.

Most of the corn America exports isn't purchased by poor countries. They don't have the money to buy it, no matter how cheap it is. Japan often purchases more U.S. corn than any other country. And when U.S. grain is cheap enough that poorer countries can buy it, the grain is so cheap, it puts local farmers from the poorer country out of business. This isn't good for local economies and can worsen their poverty.

This is a bigger deal than we might think. The vast majority of people in developing nations don't live in cities. They live in the countryside, and most of them are small farmers. Agricultural products are a large part of their country's economy.

So when grain prices drop too low, rather than helping poor people, it can and does make them even poorer. In September, 2006, for example, NPR reported that the abundant and inexpensive corn exported from the United States to Mexico harmed the Mexican farmers' ability to earn enough money.

Alexandra Spieldoch of the Institute for Agriculture and Trade Policy said, "Research shows that domestic food productivity is more effective in stabilizing developing-country food security than the reliance on inexpensive food imports. A fair price for the farmer's production will also help stabilize demand for wage labor in the local economy."

Jeffrey and Adrian Goettemoeller, experts in environmental remediation and sustainable agriculture, and authors of the book, *Sustainable Ethanol*, wrote:

> "Keeping grain prices quite low might seem like a good way to fight poverty, but the opposite result can come about when economies based largely on agriculture are damaged. Ironically, then, a reduction in U.S. exports resulting from increased corn ethanol production might help alleviate poverty-driven hunger in some places when coupled with efforts to enhance food production within developing countries."

The proliferation of farmers around the world would also, of course, produce more total food worldwide. And it globally diversifies the *sources* of food, which stabilizes the world's food production, helping to prevent the world's food supply from becoming vulnerable to a drought or a crop disease in any particular region.

In an interview with Ethanol Producer Magazine, Anne Korin and Gal Luft, the authors of *Energy Security Challenges for the 21st Century*, talk about food prices:

> Besides outlining the need for fuel choice, the authors tackle misconceptions facing corn ethanol — "the fuel the pundits love to hate." For one thing, everywhere he goes, Luft meets

misinformed people who believe that ethanol causes starvation. This myth has its roots in 2008 when ethanol faced its fiercest critics, who gave the industry a black eye by claiming biofuel was at the root of a commodity price boom. The source was an "orchestrated campaign" by Big Oil, food makers and others opposed to ethanol on the grounds that it is a waste of taxpayer money, Luft says. "All of these groups came together and helped each other and funded each other," he says. "They did huge damage to the industry."

Food companies perpetuate the myth out of resentment, Korin says. When oil prices pass a certain point, ethanol makes corn economic, she said, which means price supports for corn are no longer necessary. In that scenario the food industry has to pay market prices for corn syrup and animal feed. "Big Food for years has used underpriced corn syrup, enjoying taxpayer dollars paid as price supports to corn farmers, as a replacement for sugar, because the U.S. has a sugar quota and tariff system that keeps sugar prices much higher than elsewhere in the world," she says. "But instead of taking on the sugar lobby, Big Food has masqueraded itself as a defender of the market and the poor, in the hopes of reverting to a world in which ethanol goes away, corn price supports are required, and it gets all the underpriced corn syrup it wants."

The following is an excerpt from Gal Luft and Anne Korin's article, *Fueled Again*:

Sugar yields five times more energy than corn and costs half the price to turn into ethanol...

Unfortunately, the United States does not have an ideal climate for growing sugar cane — sugar needs a long, frost-free growing season — and is not able to ramp up sugar production to the level needed to even come close to satisfying its energy needs. This is why Latin American and Caribbean countries like Brazil, Guatemala, Honduras, the Dominican Republic, Costa Rica, El Salvador and Jamaica — all low-cost sugar cane producers — could become keys to U.S. energy security.

Brazil, the Saudi Arabia of sugar, already exports half a billion gallons of ethanol a year and could provide the United States with cheap ethanol.

"We don't want to sell liters of ethanol," Brazil's Agriculture Minister Roberto Rodrigues said in 2004. "We want to sell rivers."

Expanding U.S. fuel choice to include biofuels imported from our neighbors in the Western Hemisphere has significant geopolitical benefits at a time when U.S. standing in the region is challenged. Sugar is now grown in one hundred countries, many of which are poor. Encouraging these countries to increase their output and become fuel suppliers could have far-reaching implications for their economic development.

By creating economic interdependence with sugar-producing countries in Africa and the Western Hemisphere, the United States can strengthen its position in the developing world and provide significant help in reducing poverty.

The World Bank report by John Baffes and Tassos Haniotis entitled, "Placing the 2006/08 Commodity Price Boom into Perspective," argues that high oil prices and speculation were the primary causes of high food prices and biofuels played a very small role. To quote from the report:

"Worldwide, biofuels account for only about 1.5 percent of the area under grains/oilseeds. This raises serious doubts about claims that biofuels account for a big shift in global demand. Even though widespread perceptions about such a shift played a big role during the recent commodity price boom, it is striking that maize prices hardly moved during the first period of increase in US ethanol production, and oilseed prices dropped when the EU increased impressively its use of biodiesel. On the other hand, prices spiked while ethanol use was slowing down in the US and biodiesel use was stabilizing in the EU."

We have been given false information. Ethanol production does not cause starvation or expensive food.

Not Enough Land

Another common misrepresentation is that there is not enough farmland in the U.S. to create all the fuel we need. This is a meaningless argument if we're going to import ethanol from other countries, but let's look at what we've got. In the continental U.S. we have about 2,250 million acres of land. 1,600 million of those acres can actually be used as farmland, but not all of it is being used. In fact, only about half (800 million acres) is designated as farmland, but out of that, only 280 million acres of *that* land actually has something growing on it.

What about corn? It's a big crop. Out of the 280 million acres, 85 million is used to grow corn, but only about a fifth of *that* land (17 million acres) grows the corn that becomes ethanol.

The U.S. has all the farmland it needs to not only supply its own food and fuel but to create surplus for the rest of the world too. And that's only talking about farmland and corn.

Ethanol can be made from many other plants, municipal waste, and even natural gas and coal. And some of that, like switchgrass and miscanthus, can be grown on land that is *unsuitable* for farming.

And this is not counting fuel crops like algae and Agave that can be grown on land that cannot be used to grow even grasses — like our vast deserts — with which we can produce fuel in abundance.

The idea that we don't have enough farmland is another false notion that has entered the minds of many people without them ever knowing where it came from or where they heard it first. These ideas and many others have misled us. We have overlooked an excellent fuel that could solve many of our most challenging and important problems.

Let's look at some of the reasons alcohol is such an excellent fuel.

Why Alcohol
is a Superior Fuel

1. **Alcohol burns cooler.** One of the most significant things that stresses your car is the engine heating up to high temperatures and then cooling, over and over. Engines last longer when they burn alcohol because the car doesn't get as hot.

The two alcohol fuels likely to compete most successfully with petroleum are ethanol and methanol.

Ethanol can be made from fermentable materials; usually from sugar beets, corn, sorghum or sugarcane, although it can also be made from almost any plant material and many different kinds of waste.

Methanol can be made from plant material, or anything that ever *was* a plant. That means methanol (a fuel that burns efficiently in regular internal-combustion engines) can be made out of many things we have in abundance in America — natural gas, coal, biomass, agricultural waste, landfill gas, industrial waste and CO_2

itself — and all of this can be done right now using existing mature technologies.

Both methanol and ethanol burn cooler than gasoline. This also makes alcohol a *safer* fuel. In fact, in 1964, there was a seven-car crash at the Indianapolis 500 which killed two drivers because 150 gallons of gasoline caught fire. One of the drivers involved in the crash survived because his car was running on methanol, and it didn't ignite. In response, the United States Auto Club banned gasoline. The race cars ran on methanol exclusively for the next 41 years. In 2007, they switched to ethanol, which is also safer than gasoline for the same reasons.

2. Alcohol is a clean-burning fuel. When alcohol burns, it leaves almost no residue. Engines that have been burning alcohol since the beginning are still shiny and clean-looking after long use. They are not covered with black carbon grime as engines are when they burn gasoline.

You can demonstrate this for yourself. Take two metal coffee cans (shiny on the inside) and put a little alcohol in one and roughly the same amount of gasoline in the other. Throw a match in each one and let them burn out (do this outdoors and nowhere near anything else flammable, of course). Or watch it done on YouTube.

When they both finish burning, the inside of the alcohol can will still be clean and shiny. But the inside of the gas can will be black and sooty even after such a small amount of gasoline burned in it. Alcohol is *much* cleaner and better for your engine.

3. Alcohol fuel protects our economy. Because we can use feedstocks available within our country and make our own fuel, we can keep our economy unharmed by oil embargoes and the price manipulations of OPEC nations.

In the fuel industry, the term "feedstock" means "the raw material the fuel is made from." If ethanol is made from fermented corn, the "feedstock" is corn. If methanol is made from plant waste, the "feedstock" is plant waste.

We have so many feedstocks within our borders, we can easily make all the fuel we want without importing anything necessary for fuel.

4. It will save taxpayers money. No longer will the government have to pay for farmers *not* to grow crops (something that the government has been doing for almost a century), or to subsidize the ethanol industry at all.

Remember, the ethanol fuel industry was originally begun because grain producers were trying to find other uses for their overly-abundant crops.

With enough cars on the road capable of burning alcohols, ethanol producers will be successful enough to need no government help.

5. Alcohol made from plants greatly improves the carbon balance. Plants take in carbon dioxide (a greenhouse gas) from the air to make hydrocarbons which we then burn in our cars, releasing the CO_2 back into the air. So technically, it should all be equal. But the root hairs of the plants often stay in the soil, improving the richness of the soil and leaving some of the carbon trapped in the earth.

Critics of alcohol fuels say farmers use petroleum-fueled tractors and trucks to grow crops for ethanol so the process puts more CO_2 into the air than the plants take out. But this is a specious argument. Those tractors and trucks can and should be burning ethanol, and in some cases, they do.

6. Alcohol will lower the price at the pump. Because oil's price is artificially high, with competition by abundant, clean, homemade fuels, the oil industry will have to choose between dropping its price or losing business. And since the alcohol industries continue to improve their efficiency, fuel prices are likely to *keep* dropping, forcing oil prices lower to compete.

7. Our dollars will go further across the board. Lowering fuel prices will affect the price of almost everything else because fuel is such a large factor in the price of most goods.

8. With a greater reliance on alcohol for fuel, we'll have less need for military involvement in the Middle East. The United States military guards shipping lanes out of the Middle East. We guard our oil-producing allies there. These operations cost a lot of money and should technically be factored into the price for the gasoline we pay at our local station. If we were producing more of our fuel domestically, we could save on these military operations — saving a lot of money *and saving lives.*

According to Fuel Freedom, "The bulk of our national security budget is spent on protecting oil routes in oil-rich regions" and "the bulk of our homeland security budget is spent to protect us against petro dollar funded terrorism."

Let's recap so far. When you buy gasoline, roughly half the money stays in this country and half leaves (we import 42-60% of our oil). Out of the amount that leaves, about half goes to OPEC, including Saudi Arabia and Iran. Buying gasoline supports the spread of virulent Wahhabism and funds terrorism around the world. Using gasoline for fuel weakens our national security.

When you buy or make alcohol fuel, the money stays in America. None goes to OPEC. It puts money into our economy. The money is not concentrated in a very few superwealthy people but is more moderately earned and spent by far more people.

9. The rise of the alcohol fuel industry can help people in underdeveloped countries rise out of poverty. The ethanol industry will remove subsidies to corn farmers because they'll have a domestic market for everything they grow. That would stop American corn from undercutting local farmers in underdeveloped countries, so those local farmers will be able to make a living, which provides food and jobs for their local economy.

Also, as the alcohol fuel market grows, underdeveloped countries can grow plant material, convert it to fuel, and sell it as a compact, easily-transportable, valuable export commodity, increasing their income and improving their standard of living.

They will also, of course, be producing fuel, which means they will be able to generate their own power to fuel their own transportation, no matter how remote their location, which will also improve their standard of living. If you think the high prices that OPEC sets for oil is hard for *you*, realize that the cost of fuel is impossibly out of reach for a poor farmer in a developing nation. A booming alcohol industry could change that.

10. It is less harmful to the environment. If a tanker of ethanol spilled into the ocean, it would be gone in a few days, causing almost no damage. This is in great contrast to what happens when oil is spilled into the ocean. Burning or spilling ethanol or methanol is *far less destructive* to the environment than burning or spilling petroleum.

Because gasoline has a low octane rating, it was suggested way back in the early 1900s that ethanol (which has a naturally high octane rating) should be added to gasoline to make it burn better.

But the oil industry resisted the idea. Like an irrational sibling rivalry, the oil companies would use *anything* rather than validate the usefulness of their biggest competitor.

So they added lead to gasoline, and used it for a long time — from 1917 until 1987, when it was finally stopped because, of course, lead is poisonous.

Now ethanol is added to most gasoline routinely, and it not only reduces the toxic output of a car because alcohol itself is less polluting than gasoline, but alcohol also helps the *gasoline* burn more completely, so it lowers the amount of pollution produced from the burning gasoline too.

11. Alcohol fuel can be made from trash. This is one of the most exciting potential benefits of fuel competition in America. Every day immense amounts of perfectly good carbohydrates are thrown away in restaurants, grocery stores, donut shops, etc.

The food is thrown away because, understandably, these businesses don't want to serve stale donuts or bread, but if they give it away to hungry people and someone eats it and gets sick, the business could be legally liable. So it goes to a landfill.

Anyone who has ever worked at a grocery store or restaurant or donut shop is often *astonished* at how much perfectly good food is thrown away. Donuts from a batch made that morning and sold to customers 15 minutes before the store closed, are thrown away. A business can never predict exactly how much they are going to sell on any given day, and they don't want to cut it too close because they don't want to run out, so they routinely have too much, and when it's no longer fresh, out it goes. An estimated *one third* of all bread made in the United States is thrown away.

This could all be easily and inexpensively turned into ethanol. Fuel from trash.

You can do it yourself. You can make a regular stop at a grocery store or donut shop, collect their carbohydrate waste, and make your own fuel for very little money. When you get the feedstock for free, fuel is really inexpensive to make (to learn more about this, read David Blume's *Alcohol Can Be a Gas*).

12. Another kind of trash waste can also be made into fuel. New technologies are converting municipal waste into ethanol or methanol for fuel. Several companies have made arrangements with local municipal waste-collection services and full-scale commercial facilities are under construction. The technology has been worked out in pilot projects already. The trash is collected like it normally is, but it's then delivered to the alcohol plant instead of the landfill. The garbage is then converted into alcohol fuel and electricity. The result is far less trash ending up in landfills.

The first large-scale commercial waste-to-ethanol facility that received registration from the EPA to produce cellulosic ethanol (fuel made from cellulose — non-food waste materials like corn husks) just opened in Vero Beach, Florida in 2012. As I'm writing this, the facility is up and running, producing electricity from yard and other vegetative wastes, and agricultural wastes. And soon it will be producing ethanol fuel too. It's expected to produce six megawatts of power and eight *million* gallons of ethanol per year — out of garbage that would have been dumped in a landfill.

Scientists presented themselves with this challenge: Find a way to turn an abundantly-available non-food material into fuel and electricity without polluting the atmosphere. And they've done it.

The new facility (called Ineos Bio) uses a process called *gasification*, which heats up the garbage to 800 degrees Celsius, creating what is called *synthesis gas*, or "syngas." The heat breaks material down to core elements — hydrogen, carbon dioxide, etc. — and then Ineos Bio adds a naturally-occurring bacteria capable of quickly fermenting the hot gases into ethanol.

It requires fuel to get the process started, but once it gets going, it is self-sustaining. In other words, the heat causes new garbage to burn, which causes more heat, so they can keep shoveling in garbage, and it just keeps burning, making the temperature stay where they need it without having to add any other heat source except the garbage itself.

Excess heat from this process is fed to a steam turbine, which produces electricity, powering the facility and producing extra power, which is put onto the local electricity grid, providing electricity for an estimated 1,400 homes.

As Jim Lane, the editor of *Biofuels Digest* wrote, "It's taking landfill and turning it from a problem into an economic opportunity, and that's good for Ineos, but it's also good for Vero Beach. They're on the verge of becoming Florida's largest energy exporter, and that's a unique position for a small town."

The construction, engineering, and manufacturing of the Ineos Bio facility created 400 jobs. And it now has 60 full-time employees.

Every city should do this with their trash — make fuel from the local garbage. As the Fuel Freedom Foundation's co-founder Yossie Hollander quipped, the U.S. is "the Saudi Arabia of garbage." According to EF123, an energy funding company that specializes in waste-to-energy developments, the average American throws away about five pounds of trash *per day!*

Another similar facility is under construction in Carson City by Fulcrum Sierra Biofuels. They've got a twenty-year contract with Waste Management and Waste Collections Inc. to pick up the garbage and bring it to their facility, which will then be sorted to remove recyclable material like cans, bottles, plastics and paper. It will then annually convert what's left — 147,000 tons of municipal solid waste — into ten *million* gallons of ethanol. It is scheduled to be up and running in 2015.

Still another company in Montreal "makes ethanol from old utility poles and household garbage," says Matthew Wald, a green energy writer for the *New York Times*. The same company (Enerkem) just received a loan guarantee to build a similar plant in Tupelo, Mississippi which will consume 100,000 tons of garbage per year, transforming it into methanol. The methanol can then be converted to ethanol, or sold directly to American drivers as methanol for their cars if cars were warranted for it (the Methanol Institute is working on that).

Enerkem not only gets the feedstock (garbage) for free, they are actually getting *paid* to dispose of the garbage, making its feedstock what the company calls "cost-negative." The feedstock is readily available in abundant, uninterrupted supplies, and the infrastructure already exists to collect and deliver the "feedstock."

According to chemical engineering researchers at Fayetteville, Arkansas, 70% of municipal solid waste can be used to create fuel. They're talking about food waste, yard waste, paper, wood, and textiles. What can not be converted to fuel can be converted to electricity.

Converting this material to fuel and power is doubly beneficial, because when garbage is taken to a landfill, it's broken down by microbes into methane gas, a potent greenhouse gas (it is far better at trapping heat than CO_2), which rises to the surface and then into the atmosphere. The syngas production process prevents this from happening. The process is able to use about 90% of the waste stream, and produces minimal emissions.

If you ever hear about a local proposal for such a thing, lend your support. These projects often *need* support because they are routinely opposed. One recent project proposal in Chicago, for example, faced strong opposition from the county dump (the landfill) because, of course, the dump would lose a lot of business when the new ethanol plant opens (people *pay* to dump their stuff at landfills).

There was enough public support, however, and the ethanol plant is proceeding. Lend *your* support to such projects when you can.

This is one of the most important things we can do: Turn solid waste that would have gone into a landfill into fuel. Would you like to see more investments in waste-to-fuel facilities? All that's missing is a strong demand for ethanol and investors will line up to put their money down. It is a potentially very profitable enterprise because the facility gets their raw material for *free*, and they might even get *paid* to take it.

Let's encourage this kind of investment by creating a growing demand for ethanol fuel.

13. Here's another way to use waste to make fuel: Using cattail swamps to turn fecal sludge into clean water and clean fuel. Cattails thrive in wastewater, growing very large. Shown side by side, cattails grown in a regular swamp are big, but cattails grown in waste water are at least *twice* as big.

Cattails grow quickly and have large, starchy roots which can be mashed up and fermented to make ethanol. An acre of corn can yield 350 gallons of ethanol per year. An acre of cattails can yield a whopping *2500 gallons* according to David Hull, Karl Klingenspor, and Steven Wilbur of Wetland Engineering and Technology, and that's in cold northern areas. In a warmer climate, an operation could produce a full cattail harvest twice or three times a year!

Every city has to process sewage in some way or another. One excellent, cost effective, fuel producing way is to create a 35-acre bog filled with cattails and run the waste into it. The cattails suck up all the yuck and out the other end flows clean water into the ocean or a river.

Every city and town should have one. It is not only a great public service, it is *profitable*.

14. Yet another way to use waste: Turn air pollution into fuel. This is done by growing algae, which can be made into biodiesel, ethanol, or methanol. That is great enough by itself. But researchers found that if you feed the algae extra CO_2, the algae will grow *much* faster.

So several algae-growing facilities have been set up directly next to factories that produce CO_2 exhaust.

Normally, a factory has to go to considerable *expense* to scrub the CO_2 out of their exhaust. But with an algae facility next door, they can pump the CO_2 into the clear tubes used to grow algae and transform it into a bumper crop, absorbing the CO_2 in the process.

Most plants will grow faster if they get extra CO_2 because CO_2 is one of only three main essentials for plant life. Plants take in the CO_2, use sunlight to split carbon from the oxygen, and then combine the carbon with water to make carbohydrates (hydrated carbon). The oxygen is expelled into the atmosphere.

If a plant has plenty of water and sunlight, the limiting factor in its growth is CO_2. Well, we've got plenty of that, don't we? We can use it to make fuel.

15. Another idea is to use our deserts. Algae can be grown in ponds or clear pipes. In the deserts of the southwest United States, algae farms would get plenty of sunlight, using land not used as farmland. With only fifteen percent of the Sonoran Desert alone, algae farms could make all the fuel needed to completely replace petroleum in the United States.

These are just some of the possibilities, and these have developed without the financial incentive provided by a large alcohol fuel market. Wait until there are 100,000 alcohol fuel pumps in the U.S. Wait until we have a hundred million or more cars on the road capable of burning alcohol. We will see a prodigious bloom of invention and innovation in America. The incentive will be enormous. Hundreds of billions of dollars a year are spent on transportation fuel in America. Anyone who

can find better ways to make fuel will find eager customers.

Waste is everywhere you look — waste that can be
turned into ethanol or methanol. Mowed lawns could
be converted to fuel. Florists throw away an immense
amount of biomass. Grocery produce departments
throw away lots of potential fuel feedstock — trim-
mings from cabbage and lettuce and carrots, the fruit
and vegetables that ripen before being sold, etc. There
is plant waste everywhere, and it can all be converted
into fuel.

We could end the era of waste, and we could experience energy independence, national security, economic vitality, and a cleaner environment along with it.

But for this to happen, we need more cars on the
road that can burn alcohol. But we need not be limited
to alcohol. It may be the most *immediate* solution (it
may even be the best *long-term* solution; only time will
tell). But we should not limit ourselves here. We'll explore in the next chapter why *fuel choice* and multiple
options are the "silver bullet" everyone has been seek-
ing.

Both is Better than Either

Even though alcohol is a first rate fuel, it is not the answer. Making our cars capable of burning multiple fuels is the answer. Brazil's experience contains a lesson for us here. After the first oil embargo in 1973, Brazil, too, realized it couldn't allow its economy to remain vulnerable to the whim of OPEC, so Brazilians aimed for fuel independence.

They have an abundance of sugarcane, which can be easily and affordably turned into ethanol. Since they had a military dictatorship at the time, they were able to make drastic changes quickly: Ethanol pumps became mandatory at every fuel station, extra acres were immediately planted with sugarcane, ethanol production plants immediately began to be built, and car manufacturing facilities — and this includes the Ford and GM factories in Brazil — began cranking out cars that could run on ethanol. If any automaker wanted to sell their cars in Brazil, they had to make them capable of burning ethanol, which (fortunately for car makers) is not at all difficult to do.

But Brazil made a critical mistake: The new cars could *only* run on ethanol. They couldn't run on gasoline.

Brazil is often pointed to as an example of a country that improved its energy security and its economic growth with a domestic ethanol industry. And what Brazil accomplished is amazing. They have become independent of foreign oil in one generation. In 1975 they were dependent on foreign oil — importing *eighty percent* of their oil — and now Brazil is an oil *exporter* (*and* an ethanol exporter).

Brazil started on its ethanol program in response to the 1973 oil embargo. They kept escalating their ethanol conversion until by the mid-1980s *two thirds* of the cars made in Brazil burned only ethanol. At the time, everything was going according to plan. Ethanol was cheaper than gas. It extended the life of the car (because it burns cleaner and cooler), polluted less, and the money Brazilians spent for the fuel stayed in Brazil and boosted their economy. Everybody was happy (except the oil industry).

Then in the mid-1980s the global price of oil started dropping and stayed low throughout the 1990s — which sent over half the ethanol plants in the U.S. into bankruptcy — and what happened in Brazil? Drivers with ethanol-only cars were paying *more* for their fuel than the owners of old-fashioned gasoline-only cars!

This was a hard blow to the alcohol fuel industry. Alcohol was on the brink of becoming a serious competitor when suddenly world oil prices (still controlled by OPEC) sunk very low and stayed low for years.

Starting with the first oil embargo, both Brazil and the United States responded with heavy investments in alternative fuels. William McDonough, founder of an environmental design firm, said, "In the 70s, Sheik Yamani, speaking for OPEC in London, said, 'We will drop the price of oil, destroy those investments on Wall Street, and then put the old price of oil back' — which is exactly what they have done every single decade."

Ethanol cars went out of favor in Brazil. Everybody lost interest in alcohol fuels. Gasoline was cheap. Brazil almost entirely stopped making ethanol cars.

But with the rise of oil prices in the new millennium, Brazil came back to ethanol, but with a big improvement. Now they're using *flex fuel* cars. The cars coming out of their factories can burn either gas or ethanol or both in any proportion, giving drivers a choice, and leaving their economy far less affected by anything OPEC might do. By 2009, 94% of new cars sold in Brazil were flex fuel vehicles.

And recently they were able to officially declare their energy independence. In 2010, Brazil's economy grew *three times faster* than Britain's. In 2011, Brazil passed Britain to become the sixth largest economy in the world.

The U.S. can break free of oil's monopoly too by simply making a significant percentage of our cars flex fuel vehicles. One way to accomplish this is with a government mandate (passing an open fuel standard bill mandating that cars sold in the U.S. must be flex fuel capable). Another way is by education, a grass-roots movement and personal choice. Passing the bill *and* a grassroots movement *together* would be ideal, because even if all new cars were flex fuel, we would still have roughly 240 million gas-only cars on the road with an average life span of 15 years.

If you convert your car to a flex fuel vehicle, you will personally benefit immediately because alcohol is a superior fuel for combustion engines and you'll often pay less at the pump. At the same time, you will help bring America closer to fuel independence and economic vitality.

Fuel Competition is Mentally Healthy

I was talking with the director of a large mental health hospital a few months ago. They had just finished building a new wing of the hospital, and he said they have been extremely busy since the Great Recession began. He told me something I've never heard before — recessions always initiate a steep rise in mental health problems.

I must have looked surprised. He explained, "Well, people lose their jobs, which causes stress, and sometimes they lose their houses too. Under the strain, couples get divorced. Depression and anxiety increase. Anger and frustration rear their ugly heads. Sometimes people deal with it by drinking too much or taking drugs, and that causes even more problems. Sometimes the stress can trigger the onset of latent problems like psychosis and schizophrenia."

All of this got me to thinking. Since every time oil prices have spiked since WWII, we've had a recession in the United States, and since recessions cause more peoples' lives to fall apart, and since we could prevent rising oil prices from causing recessions if we had sufficient fuel competition, then it is not unreasonable to assert the following:

Oil's monopoly on transportation fuel causes mental illness.

Or at least the oil monopoly plays a causative role in triggering a greater number of mental health problems than would otherwise have occurred.

So we can chalk this up as yet another good reason to stop the insanity of perpetuating a one-fuel economy. In addition to increasing our national security and boosting our economy, fuel competition can help keep our citizens mentally healthy. In addition to curtailing the money going to prop up dangerous women-oppressing regimes, lowering the amount of lobbying and influence the oil industry enjoys, helping to solve our garbage and landfill problem, helping people in developing nations rise out of poverty, and reducing the amount of pollution and greenhouse gases sent into the atmosphere, into the ocean, and into the ground, fuel competition might also literally make the world a saner place.

Gasoline's Greater Range

Some people have argued against flex fuel cars or the Open Fuel Standard because methanol and ethanol don't give cars enough range. In the same sized fuel tank, a full tank of gasoline would travel more miles than a full tank of methanol or ethanol.

There are two answers to this. One is that the range difference isn't as great as you'd think — especially if the car is optimized for alcohol fuels. Most of the comparison between gasoline and alcohol uses BTUs (British Thermal Units), which is a measure of heat. Gasoline produces more heat when it burns. But heat is not what creates forward motion. Gasoline produces more heat, but some of its energy is expended in producing heat, and that energy is wasted. More of alcohol's energy is used to power the car and less of it is wasted on creating heat.

Also, alcohol fuels become more efficient at higher compression. So the difference in miles per gallon between gasoline and alcohol will be smaller with a higher compression engine. Engineers are already in the process of perfecting a variable-compression engine.

The second answer is that if it is a flex fuel car, *it doesn't matter* that alcohol doesn't have as much range as gasoline because if you're going on a long trip or want more range, *you can just buy gasoline*. The car can burn gasoline too. That's the whole point. You will have a *choice*. If you want to burn *nothing but* gasoline, no matter how expensive it gets, you will be able to. Flex fuel technology doesn't reduce a car's ability to burn gasoline. That's why so many people own flex fuel vehicles now without even knowing it: Because they've been burning gasoline in their cars and it burns gasoline just as well as a gasoline-only car.

Natural Gas is a Fossil Fuel

One of the most promising potential rivals capable of competing with petroleum in the liquid fuel market is methanol made from natural gas. But some people don't like it because it is a fossil fuel so it adds carbon to the atmosphere. I would like to offer an argument in favor of natural gas, despite its fossil fuel status:

It is being burned anyway.

When drilling for oil, natural gas comes up too. It could be captured and sold, but natural gas is now so cheap and plentiful, many producers around the world simply flare it — they burn it just to get rid of it.

A recent satellite photo shows the flaring taking place in the Bakken fields, which flares the equivalent of one fourth of all the natural gas being used in the United States. The Bakken fields are only one of many places in the U.S. doing this. And it is being done in oil fields all over the world.

If the natural gas now being flared was turned into methanol and sold at the current price of 93 cents a gallon, it could displace a lot of gasoline. At the moment, we are burning both. We're burning gasoline (a much dirtier fossil fuel) to move our cars and we're flaring off natural gas for no purpose whatsoever. If the market was opened to methanol as a liquid fuel (one of the outcomes of the Open Fuel Standard), significantly less total fossil fuel would be burned. And it would create a market for other inexpensive non-fossil fuels, like methanol made from municipal waste, which would reduce landfill bulk and pollution and decrease the burning of fossil fuels even further (using market forces rather than costly government regulation).

The Answer is Multiple Choice

People may argue methanol is better than ethanol, or only certain ways of making fuel are acceptable, or all cars should be electric or natural gas or hydrogen.

But nobody can say any one thing can replace oil. We need *all* these ways. And we need cars that can handle all sorts of fuel and power: A flex-fuel plug-in hybrid, for example.

Brazil has cars on the road that are capable of burning both compressed natural gas and gasoline, which means they could also run on ethanol, methanol and butanol, and if you made it a plug-in hybrid, you'd have a car capable of allowing six different "fuels" to compete with each other every time you fill up.

We need to approach fuel independence like our electricity grid. We need dozens of ways to power engines that move, and the more choices our vehicles have, the more powerful we are as individuals and as a nation.

Right now, ethanol-burning and electric cars are the two most competitive alternatives to gas-only cars. But if you have a gas-only car right now, you can make it a flex fuel car and begin immediately to change the world.

Raise your voice for freedom of choice so you can buy whatever fuel you prefer. Let's give ourselves multiple choices.

Imagine a day when we have as much choice with fuel as we have with coffee. Imagine going to a service station and being able to *choose* between different fuels like methanol and ethanol, and even different kinds of each. In other words, you would be able to choose ethanol made from the local waste-to-fuel plant or ethanol made from corn. Even if the corn ethanol was less expensive, many people would still choose the local waste ethanol, just as today people often pay more to buy organically grown coffee or fair trade coffee even though other coffees are cheaper.

Wouldn't it be great to be able to make these kinds of choices with *fuel?*

Will We Have Problems?

When you bring up the topic of burning alcohol fuels, people mention the many problems involved. How will we get sufficient infrastructure to support alternative fuels? Where will we get the money to build facilities that will turn waste into fuel? How can we make sure the alternative fuels can compete successfully with gasoline? How can we make sure our production of alternative fuels will be sustainable and environmentally responsible? And so on. The questions are endless.

And the questions are valid and worthwhile. But there is something over and above these questions well worth considering: That these will be *our* problems and we will be able to solve them. And all the work and investment and jobs that we create to solve the problems — these will all strengthen our economy.

But allowing our country to remain dependent on oil creates problems we can never solve.

Smart people have been earnestly trying to solve the oil dependence problem for more than forty years, and have been frustrated at every turn by the scope of the situation and the overarching control of OPEC.

But we've finally got a solution that will work. And we *know* it will work because Brazil has already done it.

Will there be problems? You bet. But they will be *our* problems. And those we can solve.

Doing What We Do Best

Critics of ethanol say that we shouldn't use food for fuel. Some scientists have said, "Okay, we'll make it out of plant waste. We'll make it out of the stalks and husks of corn and use the corn for food. We'll make it out of sawdust and tree bark, etc." Critics then said, "The technology isn't good enough. We can't make it cost effective." We just watched a half-hour documentary entitled *Energy Challenges*, that reminded us about the power of innovation.

The program discussed cellulosic ethanol — ethanol made from non-starchy, not-sugary plant material like grass and leaves. When that can be done cost-effectively, we will have alcohol fuel in such abundance, our victimization by the oil monopoly will be as good as cured. One of the biggest challenges to making cellulosic ethanol viable in the marketplace is getting the cost of the *enzymes* down low enough to make the price of the resulting fuel competitive with gasoline. The enzymes break cellulose down into sugar, so regular fermentation can take place.

In the program, one sentence both impressed us and gave us confidence that the challenge can and will be overcome. It said:

> Scientists have brought the cost of the enzymes down from five dollars per gallon of ethanol produced to *twenty cents* per gallon of ethanol produced.

That's what obscure scientists have accomplished with almost no market for the product. What do you think will happen when half the cars on the road could run on ethanol, methanol, and gasoline in any proportion?

Innovation is what America does best. With hundreds of billions of dollars to be made, you can take it to the bank that entrepreneurs will find better and better ways. And they'll be influenced by what people buy, so they'll create more and more environmentally-friendly, cost-effective ways to produce fuel once the market is there. Let's look at some examples of the kind of innovation we will see in abundance.

Boosting Food and Fuel Simultaneously

Researchers at the University of Minnesota fed algae meal (what's left over after algae is used to make biofuels) to dairy cows and discovered that this by-product of algae biofuel production worked as well or better than the high-protein alfalfa normally fed dairy cattle.

Do you know what this means? We can grow algae for fuel on land unsuitable for crops, feed it CO_2 exhaust that would normally be sent into the atmosphere (which will make the algae grow faster), make fuel out of it, and with the *leftovers*, we can replace some or all of the feed now being grown on croplands (alfalfa) to produce food.

Algae can be made into many kinds of fuel — ethanol, methanol, bio-diesel, and green crude.

Innovations like these already happen fairly often. But enough cars on the road that can burn alcohol will provide an enormous economic incentive to find ways to successfully compete with petroleum for the fuel market. Who knows what kind of breakthroughs are possible?

Ethanol Doesn't Mean Corn

In his book, *Plan B 2.0*, Lester Brown, founder of the Worldwatch Institute and the Earth Policy Institute graphed the number of gallons of ethanol per acre that can be produced with different crops. To make ethanol in the United States, most facilities use corn. But many other crops are used. How do they compare? Here's the breakdown:

Wheat: 277 gallons per acre
Corn: 354 gallons per acre
Sweet Sorghum: 374 gallons per acre
Sugarcane: 662 gallons per acre

Sugar Beets: 714 gallons per acre
Switchgrass: 1,150 gallons per acre

Sugar beets and switchgrass both require less fertilizer than corn. A research team released a report a couple months ago showing that in a genetically-altered strain, they were able to increase switchgrass's massive ethanol yield by another 38 percent!

This doesn't even *begin* to cover all the things alcohol fuels can be made from. With gasification technology (heating up organic material until the basic elements separate) we can inexpensively make alcohol fuels from wheat and barley straw, rice bagasse, municipal waste and a variety of agricultural wastes like corn stover (the stalks and husks left over after harvest), sawdust, paper pulp, small diameter trees, etc.

The greater the variety of feedstocks we use, the more energy-secure we will be. This year, corn yields may be low. Next year, maybe the switchgrass yields will be low. We need to make sure we keep our feedstock portfolio diversified for the sake of our security.

Let's not make the mistake of relying on one source of fuel. We already know what that will get us because that's what we have right now: National energy insecurity and economic instability. Let's heed the hard lesson Brazil learned and never put all our eggs in one basket again. This should be plain common sense. I hope it prevails.

Butanol Production

Several big companies, including Gevo and Butamax, have found a way to convert ethanol production facilities into butanol plants. Butanol is an alcohol with an energy density (that is, BTUs per gallon) closer to gasoline, and it is made in a way roughly similar to ethanol (using a different fermentation process) and it can be made from the same feedstocks, including corn and switchgrass.

The technology is already developed and there is a ready market — oil companies are willing to blend it with gasoline in higher percentages than ethanol, it doesn't evaporate as readily, so it can be more easily transported via pipelines. It is a promising renewable fuel.

Super Grass

A new hybrid grass has been recently developed that is *not* an invasive species, is *not* genetically modified, can be grown on *marginal* lands (land not suitable for regular agriculture) and yields more biomass per acre *than any crop ever cultivated*. It's called Giant King Grass and it grows 15-18 feet tall.

This is a fast-growing, low-cost feedstock that can be used to create ethanol, methanol and butanol, as well as what are known as "bioplastics" — a renewable replacement for petroleum-based plastics.

Fuel From the Desert

This is one of the most exciting developments in the whole biofuel field. An article in *Science Daily* said, "Scientists have found that in 14 independent studies, the yields of two Agave species greatly exceeded the yields of other biofuel feedstocks, such as corn, soybean, sorghum, and wheat."

Of course, distillers have been making tequila from Agave for a long time because its thick leaves contain a lot of sugar that can be fermented.

University of Oxford's Oliver Inderwildi, an environmental researcher, wrote: "Agave has a huge advantage, as it can grow in marginal or desert land, not on arable land." And it stands up well to extended periods of drought.

Agave plantations are already operating in Africa and Mexico, where up until now, the plant has been grown for its *fiber*.

It grows well in Australia and the American Southwest too, where vast deserts full of sunlight could provide new opportunities to grow fuel and provide incomes. Agave requires very little water.

A study published in the journal of Energy and Environmental Science discovered that ethanol made from Agave can yield an abundance of high-quality fuel with minimal impact on the environment.

Alcohol is liquid sunshine you can burn in your car. One great *advantage* to farming in the desert is the abundant sunshine. And the United States just happens to have some large deserts.

Roadside and Meridian Cropland

I was driving along the freeway yesterday and thought of an idea. On this particular freeway, as with many others, there is a significant land barrier on each side of the freeway — some thirty yards wide — plus a sizable meridian in between, all planted with trees, grasses, and bushes.

It occurred to me that this is potential energy cropland. What if it was all planted in switchgrass or miscanthus? And what if it was harvested twice a year? Harvesting in this case simply means *mowing* it. These are perennial grasses. You mow them, and they grow right back. They don't have to be continually replanted.

And since all the roots are staying in place, this would not cause soil erosion, even though it would be constantly harvested.

It would help absorb the CO_2 from the cars whizzing by, and the CO_2, in turn, would increase the plants' growth.

How many acres of meridians and roadsides do we have on the highways and freeways of America? We certainly have enough to produce a lot of fuel.

Ethanol for $1 a Gallon

Corn can produce 350-400 gallons of ethanol per acre per year. Cellulosic fuels such as grass and wood chips can produce 2,000 to 3,000 gallons of ethanol per acre per year, but so far, not cheaply enough to compete with gasoline.

But Algenol, a company in Florida, has successfully achieved 9,000 gallons of ethanol per acre per year using algae grown in salt water — at one dollar a gallon! Another company, Joule Energy, is producing 15,000 gallons of ethanol per acre per year at $1.23 per gallon using undrinkable water! And they are confident they will eventually be able to achieve 25,000 gallons of ethanol per acre per year!

How are they able to achieve this? They genetically modified algae to produce ethanol. Let me be clear: These companies are not harvesting the algae and then fermenting it. The algae itself excretes ethanol continuously, which is why the yields are so remarkable — the production is continuous year round. Corn is a crop grown and harvested only once a year.

The algae are grown inside tubes, so evaporation is minimal. It can be done in on harsh desert land — in fact that might be the best place to do it since there is so much sunlight.

To accelerate the algae's growth, waste CO_2 is pumped into it, turning a burdensome waste into a valuable resource.

What Joule Energy is doing is so remarkable, they won a very prestigious award this year by Bloomberg New Energy Finance. They said, "Every year, the Bloomberg New Energy Finance Pioneers program identifies 10 companies from around the world that are changing the energy landscape as we know it. An independent panel of industry experts from banking, academia, corporations, utilities and technology providers choose the honourees by assessing them against three criteria: potential to scale, innovation and momentum." In April, 2013, Joule was given this award.

Joule has also genetically modified algae to make diesel fuel and jet fuel.

A Waste Bonanza

And then there's all the waste, as we mentioned earlier. Many different kinds of waste can be made into fuel:

- Food processing wastes from the dairy industry, from wine and beer production, from the sugar industry, including candy factories, juice factories, etc.

- Wood from construction and demolition

- Household waste wood such as fencing and old furniture

- Municipal solid waste

- Wood waste from packaging (like crates and pallets)

- Sewage sludge

- Market waste such as unsold vegetables and green tops from grocery stores

- Gardening wastes like leaves, small branches, grass cuttings, etc.

All these sources should be *used* instead of piling up in landfills and sending methane into the atmosphere. Already, even in the absence of a strong demand for alcohol fuels, scientists and entrepreneurs have found profitable ways to make fuel from waste. This could be greatly expanded if we had fuel competition.

Americans have an enterprising and innovative culture. Especially when there is profit to be made, this feature of our society expresses itself with zeal. We're also an idealistic culture and we love to do things that benefit the planet. So once the fuel market opens up, Americans will go into overdrive finding ways to make fuels ever cleaner and cheaper, which will force gas prices lower and lower in order to compete.

And if oil prices rise, as they have lately, what will happen? Domestic producers of ethanol and methanol will work overtime to provide us with less expensive fuels, whether those fuels come from algae or municipal waste or corn stover or sugar beets or whatever. Whole industries will be scrambling as fast as they can to make and deliver fuels that cost less than gas.

What happens now (with our lack of competition at the pump) when fuel prices rise? Do our enterprising, innovating industries kick it into gear and scramble to do anything? No. There is nothing for them to do. Our cars aren't warranted to burn their fuel. They stand by, completely helpless, as more than a billion dollars a day flows out of our economy to foreign bank accounts while we pay outrageous prices for transporttation fuel.

When we have fuels freely competing at the pump, we will see the dawning of a new day. We will see the beginning of the end of oil's strategic status. And we will have a new birth of American independence.

Why Fuel Competition
is Urgent

Lowering fuel prices at the pump, reducing land-fill waste and improving the environment are wonderful benefits of robust fuel competition. But there is a critical and pressing side-effect of our lack of competition that makes this issue not only important but *urgent*. In Robert Zubrin's book, *Energy Victory*, the preface to the paperback edition makes our precarious situation painfully clear.

The hardcover came out in 2007 and the preface to his paperback was written in 2009. In that short time, a lot had happened.

In 2007, the price of petroleum was $70 a barrel. OPEC restricted its oil production and the price of oil climbed to $140 per barrel. People ran out of money so they couldn't pay their mortgages, and the housing market collapsed.

Auto sales collapsed too, for the same reason. "So, as a result of this massive new tax on our economy," as

Zubrin put it, the United States was driven into a recession. He calls it a "tax" because it is an increased cost without increased value returned, charged to anyone who drives, which is just about everyone in the United States.

It was bad enough for Americans. It was far worse for people in poorer countries who didn't have "disposable income" to dispose of.

The damage to the world's economy was caused deliberately, and I think it's important to understand this. During November and December of 2008, as many countries were trying desperately to keep their economies afloat with stimulus programs, OPEC decided *that* was the time to restrict their production, *reducing* the amount of oil on the world market by 4.5 million barrels of oil a day in order to get oil prices back up over $70 a barrel (prices had come down temporarily because the economy had fallen apart).

The American economy is dangerously vulnerable to OPEC's price manipulation.

OPEC's plans are clear — they will raise the price of oil, gouging and looting the world's economy, and that will be followed by a recession or depression, and when the economy recovers, they will continue their gouging and looting. They started with the oil crisis in the early 1970's and they've been at it ever since.

With each round of looting, the transfer of wealth from the free world to the dictators and monarchs (and the America-hating fundamentalists they support) takes another leap forward.

This is why creating a flex fuel nation is not merely a good idea — it is a burning imperative.

Every year, more and more cars on the road are flex fuel vehicles. And it is certainly possible that *eventually* most new cars would be FFVs (flex fuel vehicles), but we're like a patient in "critical condition." We are hemorrhaging our wealth, and hostile regimes are using that wealth to undermine us further — as fast as they can. We don't have the time to meander.

OPEC money is not only buying up U.S. corporations. "They are also buying up US government debt," writes Zubrin, "which recession-driven deficit spending has sent completely out of control. And with each takeover, bailout, or investment operation — or generous donation to a university or political think tank — the power and influence of the cartel's money within the American and European political systems is growing, a trend that will make effective government action to counter OPEC increasingly difficult to achieve."

OPEC has been at it for three decades. "Each looting cycle makes the enemy stronger and ever better positioned to confound our efforts to escape," says Zubrin.

Saudi Arabia at the Center

The country with the most influence within OPEC is Saudi Arabia because their oil is the cheapest of any of them. And they have the largest known reserves.

So if the cartel decides on a particular production quota for the member nations of OPEC, and one of the members decides to get greedy and exceeds their quota to take advantage of high oil prices, Saudi Arabia can raise their own oil production so dramatically that they crash world oil prices by flooding the market with excess oil. This doesn't hurt Saudi Arabia very much — they still make money because their oil is so cheap to produce. But it hurts all the rest of the member nations of OPEC.

So Saudi Arabia largely controls what OPEC does. And OPEC controls the global price of oil. And the price of oil controls the world's economy because 95% of all transportation in the world — cars, trains, ships, trucks, and planes — can run on nothing but oil, and transportation underlies the world's economy. If goods can't move around, the economy comes to a halt.

That means Saudi Arabia controls the world's economy. And they manipulate oil prices in a way that gives them the maximum amount of income, like a parasite that drains as much blood from its victim as it can, short of killing the host. Saudi Arabia has been reaping one bonanza after another for a long time. They are overflowing with money. I'm sure you've seen photos of Dubai and Riyadh. People ooh and ahh over the amazing structures, the opulence, the splendor that gouging the world affords them, without realizing that *we* paid for that. People around the world are struggling, social programs are being cut, people are losing their houses, losing their jobs while we pay at least double what we should be paying for fuel so that rich sheiks can waste their money showing off to the world. Money is drained from the free world to support all this.

"The resulting transfer of wealth," writes Gal Luft, "is already creating a structural shift in the global economy, causing oil importers economic dislocations such as swollen trade deficits, loss of jobs, sluggish economic growth, inflation and, if prices continue to soar, inevitable recessions. The impact on developing countries, many of which still carry debts from the previous oil shocks of the 1970's, is much more severe."

Adding to this transfer of wealth is terrorism. Al Qaeda has explicitly made attacking oil supplies their goal, calling oil "the provision line and the feeding to the artery of the life of the crusader's nation." From 2004 to 2008, attacks on oil fields in Iraq alone prevented one to two million barrels of oil from entering the world market, which kept the oil market $20-25 per barrel higher than it would have been otherwise.

This extra "tax" on the economies of Europe and the United States from terrorist attacks on oil facilities added up to an additional $65 to $85 billion dollars a year leaving Western economies. Terrorists have attempted to disable Abqaiq (in Saudi Arabia), the largest oil processing facility in the world. Several attempts to drive explosive-filled trucks and planes into Abqaiq were luckily thwarted. Had they been successful, they could have easily "sent oil to above $200 a barrel for an extended period of time," wrote Luft, "causing incalculable economic losses and a far greater transfer of wealth to Middle Eastern governments."

So OPEC's price-fixing manipulations and terrorists' attacks have given Saudi Arabia a rapidly increasing windfall. They're using the money to promote

Wahhabism — a dangerous, fundamentalist version of Islam.

"Until the Saudis started racking up billions in inflated oil revenues in the 1970s," wrote Zubrin, "the Wahhabi movement was regarded by Muslims the world over as little more than primitive insanity. Without rivers of treasure to feed its roots, this horrific movement could neither grow nor thrive." He writes,

> It is the Saudis' unlimited funds...that have allowed them to buy up the faculties of the Islamic world's leading intellectual centers; to build or take over thousands of mosques; to establish thousands of radical madrassas, pay their instructors, and provide the free daily meals necessary to entice legions of poor village boys to attend. Those boys are indoctrinated with the idea that the way to get into paradise is to murder Christians, Jews, Buddhists, Taoists, and Hindus (not to mention moderate Muslims)...Meanwhile, Arab oil revenues have underwritten news outlets that propagandize hatefully against the United States and the West, supported training centers for terrorists, paid bounties to the families of suicide bombers, and funded the purchase of weapons and explosives. We have been subsidizing a war against ourselves.

Saudi Arabia comprises less than two percent of the Muslim world, and yet, as I said earlier, they are financially responsible for an unbelievable *ninety percent* of all

Islamic organizations in the world! Stuart Levey, the U.S. Undersecretary of the Treasury, in charge of combating terrorist financing, said, "If I could snap my fingers and cut off the funding from one country, it would be Saudi Arabia."

And there's more. "Iran is now using its petroleum lucre to fund its nuclear program and to insulate itself from economic sanctions imposed on it," wrote Zubrin. "Once produced, Iranian nuclear weapons could be used by the Iranian regime itself or be made available to terrorists to attack U.S., European, Russian, or Israeli targets. This is one of the gravest threats to international peace and stability — and, again, we are paying for it ourselves with oil revenue.

"Our responses to these provocations have been muted and hapless because any forceful action on our part against nations like Saudi Arabia and Iran could result in the disruption of oil supplies that the world economy is utterly dependent upon. We cannot stand up to our enemies because we rely upon them for the fuel that is our economic lifeblood. We pay them for their oil and they make war on us."

While she was the U.S. Secretary of State, Condoleezza Rice said, "We do have to do something about the energy problem. I can tell you that nothing has really taken me aback more, as Secretary of State, than the way that the politics of energy is...warping diplomacy around the world. It has given extraordinary power to some states that are using that power in not very good ways for the international system — states that would otherwise have very little power."

Funding the Repression of Women

Massive oil revenues prop up repressive regimes like Saudi Arabia and Iran, who have, for all intents and purposes, *enslaved* their women. I don't think this is overstating the case. While it's true that Saudi Arabia is the only country in the world where women are not allowed to drive a car and where women are treated like second class citizens, not allowed to go anywhere alone (which is bad enough), it's much worse than that.

Human Rights Watch, in their 2012 report, said "The Saudi guardianship system continues to treat women as minors. Under this discriminatory system, girls and women of all ages are forbidden from traveling, studying, or working without permission from their male guardians."

Yakin Ertürk, Special Rapporteur from the United Nations, reported that in Saudi Arabia, if a woman is fully covered or doesn't have an ID card officials may require her to have a guardian present, which makes it almost impossible for women to make official complaints against the guardians themselves.

In a BBC article, Princess Basma Bint Saud Bin Abdulaziz, the daughter of King Saud (the former ruler of Saudi Arabia) wrote about divorce laws, "Today in Saudi, women are either at the mercy of their husbands or at the mercy of judges who tend to side with the husbands." She said it is extremely difficult for a woman to initiate divorce. It is up to the man to decide on a divorce.

And the custody of children over the age of six is automatically granted to the husband. And then there is the "Al Dali" law. "'Al Dali' is a sentence imposed by a judge whereby a man can stop his daughter, sister, cousin or whoever from doing anything she wants to do in life, be it marrying, working etc," says the princess. "There has even been known examples of it being used to divert a woman's salary so that it goes directly to her father's bank account."

In their educational system, girls are forbidden to participate in physical education. And in school, kids are "taught that a woman's position in society is inferior."

She also says that if a woman is abused by her husband, the only place she can go is the state-provided refuges. But there the women are told they have "brought shame on their families" and if their families are powerful, they are "sent straight back to their homes."

This is *slavery*. It's more than discrimination. These women do not have the freedoms their fellow male citizens have. The Saudi government uses the wealth they gain through massive oil sales to keep their regimes going, to pay for the standing army, police and weapons, to run their government and pay off their male citizens.

They produce the oil for $1.50 a barrel and through an illegal price-fixing scheme, sell it to the world for $100 a barrel or more. And because we have so far failed to introduce competition into the fuel market, we are paying for all this repression of women, handing over our money and feeling helpless to do anything about the fact that *they* are setting the price of our fuel and *they* are deciding where that money goes.

Because so many of their citizens are on the dole (the Saudi government uses their excessive oil profits to pay their citizens), more than eight million migrant workers are imported to do the jobs Saudis won't do. But the "sponsorship" system in Saudi Arabia gives control of the migrant workers' residency permits *to the employer.* A migrant worker cannot change jobs or leave the country without the *employer's* permission.

Human Rights Watch says in their 2012 report, "As in years past, Asian embassies reported thousands of complaints from domestic workers forced to work 15 to 20 hours a day, seven days a week, and denied their salaries. Domestic workers, most of whom are women, frequently endure forced confinement, food deprivation, and severe psychological, physical, and sexual abuse...In December 2010, authorities made no attempt to rescue an Indonesian migrant domestic worker who had worked for 10 years without pay and whose sponsors were 'renting' her out to other houses..."

Again, this is *slavery.* And *we* are contributing to it every time we fill our tanks with gasoline. We've been unwittingly filling our tanks with slavery, oppression, hatred, and murder. Our cars are fundraising machines and we've been donating our money to cruel men with cruel purposes. Each of us should look into our hearts and find a way to stop personally contributing to Saudi Arabia, and by doing so help bring forth a viable in-dustry that could greatly curtail their power by permanently stripping oil of its strategic status and weakening the Kingdom's ability to prop up its regime.

The second most powerful country in the OPEC cartel has traditionally been Iran. In 2010, the World Economic Forum, in their Gender Gap report, said that in Iran, women do not have equal inheritance rights and they can't be granted "guardianship rights" for their own children, even after the death of their husband. When women activists try to do something about the inequalities, the government targets them with harassment and imprisonment.

In an article in the *New York Times* about Iran, Nazila Fathi writes, "Girls can legally be forced into marriage at the age of 13. Men have the right to divorce their wives whenever they wish, and are granted custody of any children over the age of 7. Men can ban their wives from working outside the home, and can engage in polygamy. By law, women may inherit from their parents only half the shares of their brothers. Their court testimony is worth half that of a man. Although the state has taken steps to discourage stoning, it remains in the penal code as a punishment for women who commit adultery. A woman who refuses to cover her hair faces jail and up to 80 lashes."

In Iran, a law was passed that bans women (but not men) from studying 77 specific college majors, including engineering, nuclear physics, and computer science. The new policy began September 22, 2012. Iranian human rights lawyer Shirin Ebadi says it's part of Iran's policy to weaken the role of women in Iranian society. "The Iranian government," she says, "is using various, different initiatives to restrict women's access to education and to return them to the home to weaken the feminist movement in the country."

Every time you fill your tank with gas, you strengthen these nations. You give them more power to repress women and to spread their ideology to the rest of the world. Every dollar that leaves the free world to pay for OPEC oil weakens us and strengthens them. Every tank of gas threatens women's rights around the world.

We all need to get this reality to *penetrate*. We need to have these hard facts come to mind when we're filling up our tanks, and to strengthen our resolve to put a stop to it with a sense of urgency appropriate to the situation. It's bad enough as it is. But it's getting worse.

Save the King Foundation

Saudi Arabia has a problem. Their population is growing rapidly, but Saudi citizens do not pay an income tax. The government runs on oil money. And the House of Saud basically pays off their subjects to keep them from rebelling, especially after the recent uprisings in Libya, Syria and Egypt.

After the "Arab Spring" began, Saudi King Abdullah handed out pay raises, pension increases, and subsidies, almost *doubling* the Kingdom's budget. Before this began, Saudi Arabia required the world price of a barrel of oil to be about $70 or higher to pay all its bills. But after all the pay raises and increased pensions and subsidies, by 2015, they will need a barrel of oil to cost $110 or more. People keep expecting gas prices to go back down to "normal." Saudi Arabia can no longer afford that, so it is extremely unlikely that we'll ever see those prices again, unless it is a temporary measure to kill a budding fuel-industry competitor.

As Gal Luft put it, "Like it or not, the bill for keeping the Persian Gulf monarchies in power is now being footed by every American. Every time we fuel our car we send an extra 35 cents per gallon, or roughly $6 per fill up, to the Save the King Foundation. Since oil goes into everything we buy from food to plastics, this adds about $1,500 annually to the expenditures of the average American family."

"Paradoxically," says Luft, "we are forced to fund social programs for other nations at the very same time we are engaged in a heated debate about cutting social services and entitlement programs at home."

Our entire economic health is inextricably tied to the world price of a barrel of oil. So OPEC has *de facto* control over the American economy. This is a perfect formula for national insecurity.

But we can free our economy from OPEC's control right here and now. Once we create a demand for alcohol fuels, competition will begin to arrive all over America at our filling stations. The almost total reliance of our transportation vehicles on oil alone will begin to diminish, and as it does, our economy's vulnerability to OPEC's price manipulations will diminish right along with it.

That's why fuel competition is *urgent*. The longer we pay OPEC's prices, the more dangerous and oppressive the world will become. The sooner we strip oil of its strategic status, the sooner these oppressive governments will have to change, and the sooner our own economy will begin to thrive again.

There may eventually be other technologies that replace liquid fuel altogether. Maybe hydrogen. Maybe compressed natural gas. As batteries improve and become cheaper, electric cars may be the next generation. But, according to Gal Luft, "mass market penetration of battery operated vehicles will take a long time. Such cars are projected to account for only 5 percent of vehicle sales in 2020. Not until 2040 will market penetration be deep enough to make a dent in the price of oil."

Marc Rauch wrote, "At the SAE (Society of Automobile Engineers) World Congress meeting…a group of automaker representatives voiced their collective opinion that internal combustion engines — versus electric — would continue to dominate new vehicle manufacturing for at least the next two decades. This confirms what we at The Auto Channel have been saying for the past few years…"

We cannot wait until those technologies develop and become inexpensive enough to be common. In the last seven years, Americans purchased nearly 100 million new cars, and *almost all of them* were petroleum-only cars. And most cars stay on the road about fifteen years. We don't have that kind of time! Something must be done *now*, using the cars we already have and the infrastructure already in place. The cars we *have* are internal combustion engines, which burn alcohol very well.

As soon as possible, we need to break oil's monopoly on transportation. The fastest, least expensive, most immediately effective way to strip petroleum of its strategic status is with flex fuel cars — by making the cars themselves a platform upon which fuels can compete.

A Key Distinction

We have two very different ways fuels can compete with each other. One is what we have now — different cars competing with each other, each car using a single source of power: gasoline *or* compressed natural gas *or* electricity *or* hydrogen, etc. The other way to create competition is for the cars themselves to be capable of using multiple power sources, like flex fuel cars, plug-in hybrids, Ford's new F-150 that can burn both CNG and gasoline, etc.

Competition *between cars* is feeble. It is weak, slow, expensive, and cumbersome. It will do very little to lower fuel prices. Competition between power sources within a single vehicle, on the other hand, is robust, vigorous, agile and immediate. It pits fuels against each other, creating a strenuous daily battle to provide the best deal for the consumer. That's the kind of competition we should be aiming for.

To brew coffee at home, imagine what it would be like if each different kind of coffee required *a different kind of machine*. If you wanted to brew Folder's coffee, you had to use a Folder's machine. If you wanted to make Peet's coffee at home, you had to use a Peet's coffee machine. Each machine costs, let's say, $100. You would be able to say that *technically* the different kinds of coffees are competing with each other, but it is also clear that this is a far cry from what we have now — where a single drip coffee machine can brew any of these brands of coffee, which forces the brands to compete more directly with each other. They must constantly try to outcompete each other to get your coffee dollars.

What if Peet's dropped the price of their coffee, and you really liked Peet's coffee, but you had a Folder's machine? You couldn't take advantage of the new low price for Peet's unless you forked over 100 bucks for a new machine. You might hesitate to get the new machine. Peet's new lower price might be temporary, after all. And how long would it take for you to recoup the 100 dollars for the new machine at Peet's new low price?

That's the choice people have now with cars and fuels (but with far more money at stake). You can buy a CNG car right now, but not only is the car more expensive than a gasoline-only car, it still runs on only one fuel. No fuel choice. And what happens if natural gas prices rise and/or gasoline prices drop? You couldn't very easily switch to the less expensive fuel. That's what happened in Brazil during the mid-80s and early 90s — the country had switched most of their cars to ethanol-*only* cars in the early 80s (flex fuel cars hadn't been invented yet), but OPEC decided to drop the price of gasoline very low in the mid-80s. Brazilian drivers of ethanol-only cars were now paying *more* for their fuel than the owners of the old fashioned gasoline-only cars.

Competition between *cars* is feeble compared to competition between *fuels* within a single car. Think about what happened with cell phones. Originally, each cell phone had different features, and you could choose between phones. This was *weak* competition because phones cost money and you often had to agree to a two-year contract.

Now most phones are capable of using apps. The apps are competing within each phone, and innovation has *exploded*. You don't have to buy a new phone or sign a new contract to get a new function. There are literally *millions* of apps available, doing every conceivable thing, and the level of innovation is rising exponentially.

The same thing could happen in the fuels market. Imagine automakers creating cars that can use multiple power sources — the more power sources the better. For example, General Motors is coming out with a Chevrolet Impala in 2015 that will be capable of using gasoline or compressed natural gas. It will have two different tanks. Drivers will be able to fuel up on either, so those two fuels will have to compete against each other at the pump. Right now CNG is about half the cost of gasoline per mile.

But GM could go even further. Since the car can burn gasoline, with a few very minor tweaks it could also burn ethanol, using the same liquid fuel tank used for the gasoline. Now all *three* fuels would have to constantly battle each other.

When the EPA changes its regulations, methanol could be added too. *Four* fuels in a single car, and if there were enough of them on the road, those fuels would be constantly pitted against each other in fierce competition. That's starting to look like robust competition.

Methanol and ethanol can also be made from *multiple feedstocks*, and those *sources* would have to compete with each other too. Most methanol, for example, is made from natural gas. But it can be made out of many things. If a local waste conversion facility was turning garbage into methanol, it could compete with methanol made from natural gas. They could compete on price, and they could also compete on other factors. Even if the methanol made from local waste was more expensive, some people would rather buy it because it is local or because they want to support that industry, or for whatever reason. So even between different *sources* of methanol, we could have competition. The same would be true for ethanol.

But we can go still further. If the car can burn compressed natural gas and gasoline and methanol and ethanol, it might also be a plug-in hybrid. Now all those fuels would have to compete directly with electricity.

The point of all of this is that we need to draw a clear distinction between *vehicle* competition and *fuel* competition. They are two very different things. And we should be aiming most intently at *fuel* competition. We should aim at pitting fuels against each other in real time.

Methanol sells today for 93 cents a gallon. It is only 60 percent of the energy density of gasoline, but that still makes it half the cost of gasoline per mile driven. This low cost is in the absence of a vigorous competitive fuel market. If methanol was allowed to fight for our fuel dollars in an open market (which is what the Open Fuel Standard would accomplish), methanol could get even cheaper, and gasoline would have to radically drop its price if it had any hope of competing.

Robust fuel competition would transform our economy. Each of us would have more money to spend, which would create more jobs. The strategic importance of the Middle East would dwindle, which would allow for fewer conflicted foreign policy decisions. We'd save billions that we now spend protecting shipping lanes for oil. Every power source we've mentioned — CNG, ethanol, methanol, and most sources of electricity — are not only sourced in America, but they produce less pollution than petroleum fuels, so the competition would be good for our health too. The petroleum industry would no longer have a monopoly and the excessive power it gives them. America would be a happier, freer, more prosperous country.

To bring about fuel competition as quickly as possible, we should all, as well as we can, stop burning petroleum fuels and spend as much of our transportation money as we can on *anything* but oil. Right now, ethanol is the most available alternative, so we can start there.

And we should pass a national open fuel standard bill to speed up the process of making this a flex fuel nation. That's what we can do collectively.

Now let's go into more detail about what you can personally do to help turn things around.

What You Can Do
To Free Us All

In an article in *USA Today*, Wendy Koch tried to answer the question: If American oil production has risen and if we are using less oil (and both are true), then why hasn't that brought gas prices down? Her first answer is exactly right: "U.S. gas prices are largely determined by global crude oil prices." And the global price of oil isn't much affected by what the U.S. does.

Koch goes on to list five factors that influence the price of gasoline. Here they are:

1. Global crude oil price increases.
2. Iran and other geopolitical uncertainties.
3. Limited spare capacity.
4. Rising worldwide demand.
5. Refinery closures/production costs.

These are the typical reasons for high gas prices that most analysts and writers and even presidents will tell you. But I want you to notice something: We can't do much about these. Most of them we can do *nothing at all* about. And also notice that even if we did everything we could about all five of them, it *still* wouldn't bring gas prices down. This kind of "analysis" wastes our time and takes us off track.

If you concern yourself with reasons for a problem — reasons you can't do anything about — volumes of writing will accomplish exactly nothing. You might as well remain silent.

Let's look at losing weight to see how this works. Let's say I am gaining weight and I don't like it. I could talk about how our American society encourages over-eating, how advertising influences me, my family history, the dangers of supersizing, all the temptations of fast food joints, blah blah blah.

All of those things may be true, but if the goal I want to achieve is a slimmer body, these reasons are pointless for me to concern myself with. I'm not going to do much about any of them. And even if I did everything I could about all of them, *it would not help me lose weight.*

People who successfully lose weight look at it differently. They look at causes they themselves can do something about — how much they exercise, what they eat, how they handle their stresses, how much sleep they're getting, etc. All of these factors are in their personal control, and they can *do something* about all of them, and if they did it well enough, they could lose weight.

None of Koch's reasons for high gas prices help us do anything to change our plight. But there are plenty of reasons we can talk about that we *can* do something about. The fundamental determining factor causing gas prices to rise or fall is how much OPEC decides to limit its oil production.

We can limit the cartel's influence on our gas prices by breaking the monopoly and stripping oil of its strategic status. And we can get out of the box of *gas* prices and concern ourselves with *fuel* prices. How can we lower fuel prices? We can introduce competition into the fuel market by turning the cars on our roads into platforms upon which fuels can compete.

And we don't have to rely on any other country's cooperation. We can do this ourselves. OPEC may decide to continue trying to plunder the world's financial resources by keeping the price of oil high, but it would no longer affect fuel prices in America. Our fuel prices could steadily drop as we develop better ways of making fuel.

We could rely on our own resources and our own ingenuity and our own enterprising nature, and we could stop worrying that "rising worldwide demand" or "global crude oil price increases" or "Iran and other political uncertainties" will cripple our economy or even limit our travel plans.

The best way to approach the causes of *any* problem is to focus on the causes you can actually do something about.

Are you ready to get down to business?

Let's Make it Happen

Below is a list of practical actions you can take to move the United States closer to fuel independence, to limit money going to dangerous women-oppressing regimes, to lower the amount of lobbying and influence the oil industry enjoys today, to revitalize the American economy, to improve our national security, to help solve our garbage and landfill problem, to prevent mental illness, to help people in developing nations rise out of poverty, and to reduce the amount of pollution and greenhouse gases sent into the atmosphere, into the ocean, and into the ground.

1. Make your own car a flex fuel vehicle as soon as possible. Of course, you can't have any choice in fuels until your vehicle can burn more than one fuel.

The more cars on the road capable of burning alcohol, the more incentive fuel stations have for installing alcohol pumps. By making *your* car a flex fuel vehicle, you are helping to make fuel choice available to others, and you can immediately become part of the solution.

Many online stores now sell converter kits you can install yourself:

AlcoholCanBeAGas.com

Change2E85.com

Ez85.us

FlexFuelUS.com

JonnyEnergy.com

BioEtun.com

Converter kits are very easy to install. You can find videos on YouTube showing how to do it yourself. Or you can let your mechanic do it for you (the kit comes with instructions).

The converter kit essentially upgrades your fuel injector so it can handle alcohol. It usually costs less than $100 per car cylinder.

You may have heard that converting your car is illegal. That's because the Environmental Protection Agency (EPA) has prohibitions against tampering with your car's engine in a way that might alter its emissions. The law was designed to prevent *increasing* your emissions. The EPA has discovered, however, that converting a car to an FFV *reduces* emissions. Here is what the EPA says about conversions:

> It is technically possible to convert a conventional gasoline vehicle to run on E85; however, such conversions may be in violation of the anti-tampering prohibition of the Clean Air Act unless they are certified by the U.S. Environmental Protection Agency (EPA). In addition, converting a conventional vehicle to E85 may violate the terms of the vehicle warranty.

You can find more information about the EPA's position on converting your car here:

http://www.epa.gov/otaq/fuels/renewablefuels/docu ments/420f10010a.pdf

The "Smart Box" conversion kits you will find on FlexFuelUs.com are, in fact, certified by the EPA. Several of the companies we have listed above sell kits by FlexFuelUs.com. Look on the web sites for more information. It is completely legal for you to install an EPA-approved kit in your gasoline-only car, turning it into a flex fuel vehicle.

Here's a complete list of documents from the EPA about conversion kits. This will tell you pretty much anything you'd want to know about it:

http://www.epa.gov/otaq/consumer/fuels/altfuels/al tfuels.htm

Driving a flex fuel car and burning E85 instead of gasoline is by far the most meaningful and important thing you can do. Every car converted to a flex fuel vehicle makes us that much less vulnerable to oil shocks. Every tank of alcohol fuel is money taken away from the oil industry and invested in a clean, renewable, domestic industry. Every car makes a difference. Every *tank* makes a difference.

We converted our car. Klassy did it. It took about a half hour.

She watched a YouTube video showing how it was done, and she did it without any help. We immediately got into the car and took it for a drive. It ran perfectly, the computer still worked great, the onboard mileage meter worked, and no engine light came on. (We were told the car's computer might have trouble figuring out what changed, but we had no problem from the start.)

We drove it for months with the conversion kit, burning E85 (85% ethanol, 15% gasoline) and the car didn't run any differently, except it had a little more pickup when accelerating (because of the higher octane).

This is the first and most important thing you can do: Convert your own car. Then convince everyone you know to do it too. And never own a gasoline-only car again. Gasoline-only cars are bad for you and bad for the world.

It only takes half of us. Some people will not want to convert their cars or don't have even the small amount of money it takes to convert their cars to flex fuel vehicles. But we don't need everyone. If only *half* of us ran on an alcohol fuel, our problem is solved. Not only do we only import roughly half our oil, but the strong competition from alcohol — even from only half the market — would force *all* fuel prices lower, which would lower the price of almost everything.

And you may not even need a conversion kit. Several people, including Marc Rauch, the co-founder of The Auto Channel, the largest independent automotive information resource in the world, says that he has been experimenting with putting E85 into non-flex-fuel cars, and so far they have all run fine.

Automakers often give him cars to test drive and review, and after he does his test drive, he routinely puts E85 in the tank to see what happens. Usually the engine light will come on because, he says, "the cars' sensors detected something different" but the car runs great, and when he puts gasoline back in the tank, the engine light goes off again.

He knew these weren't good enough tests, so he made sure the next car he bought was a non-flex-fuel vehicle, and whenever he can, he puts E85 in it. He got a conversion kit at the time he got his car and decided to run the car without it until he had a problem, at which time he would install the kit. He's been driving it for a year and a half (25,000 miles) and has yet to put the kit on. The car is running fine, even though the engine light is always on.

Marc says he broke it in gently because David Blume, author of *Alcohol Can Be a Gas*, told him ethanol is a solvent and tends to clean the gunk out of your gas tank and fuel lines, and you don't want it all to get dissolved at once or it will clog your fuel filter. So Marc followed this advice, and had no problems.

Just to make sure there really wasn't a problem with his car, Marc brought it to a car care center and asked about the engine light. Their tests showed that the oxygen sensor had gone out. Marc then went and filled his car with regular gasoline and when the engine light went off, he went back for another test. Now the oxygen sensor wasn't broken any more.

In fact, nothing was ever broken. The car was working perfectly.

Car companies claim that they use different components in their gas-only cars than in their flex fuel cars. Ohio Biosystems tested this claim by looking at the part numbers for models of cars that have a flex fuel version and a gas-only version. They checked the fuel tanks, fuel pumps, and fuel injectors. The part numbers for the two different versions of each model *were the same*. Ohio Biosystems was kind enough to post their findings online, which you can see here:

http://www.ohiobiosystems.org/OBSC-NTEP_files/frame.htm

Robert Zubrin conducted an experiment on his 2007 Chevy Cobalt (a non-flex-fuel vehicle) to see if he could get better than 24 miles per gallon burning 100% methanol. In the process, he found discovered something interesting. As he wrote later:

> While not a flex-fuel car, the Cobalt uses the same E-37 computer and the same engine as GM's HHR, which is a flex-fuel car. In fact, all GM cars sold in the U.S. for the past five years use either the E-37 (for small cars) or the equally flex-fuel-capable E-38 (for larger cars), and so all are capable of flex-fuel operation provided they are programmed correctly. The same is true at Ford, whose cars, whether flex-fuel or not, indiscriminately use the same "black oak," "green oak," or "silver oak" computers. Without question, the same must be the case for European and Japanese cars as well, since all are sold in Brazil, where flex-fuel capability is mandatory.
>
> There was a time when adding flex-fuel capability to an automobile increased its cost by about $100. This is no longer true. Now

almost all new cars already have flex-fuel hardware, and could easily be marketed as flex-fuel vehicles.

We had an opportunity to experiment with this. In order to fix an unrelated problem with our car, we took off the conversion kit (temporarily, we thought) but in the process, we broke one of the conversion kit's plugs. So we decided to gather up some courage and try E85 without a kit just to see what would happen. We were watching a video by David Blume where he says he once mentioned on a national talk show that anyone could put E85 in their regular car, and immediately the petroleum industry made it mandatory for all gas stations to put stickers on their E85 pumps warning people not to put E85 into non-flex-fuel cars. Blume's reassurance that you can put E85 into any car (and that it's perfectly legal) was the final straw for us.

We decided to do it. We thought we'd try it in stages. So first we waited until our tank was pretty empty and put in one gallon of E85. By our calculations, that meant we were running on 33% alcohol. We figured if there was a problem, we had plenty of room in the tank to fill up with regular gasoline and dilute the ethanol enough to stop whatever problem it was causing. But we didn't have any problems. We couldn't even tell the difference. Our 2001 Prius was successfully burning E33! This was encouraging.

The next phase of our experiment was to let the tank empty out some more. Then we put in *three* gallons of E85. By our calculations that made it E70 (70%

ethanol in the tank). We still had enough room to add four more gallons of regular gasoline if there was a problem, which would have brought it back down to about E30, and we already knew the car could handle that.

But again, there was no problem. We couldn't tell any difference. The car was running perfectly! We drove around quite a bit, using up most of the tank. Everything was going smoothly.

This was great. Then we embarked on a 500-mile trip and on our way out of town, we filled up with E85, which put us at probably E80 or so. While we were at the station, we looked carefully at the little warning sticker. It said we should check with the clerk before putting E85 in our car. So we went in to see what the clerk would say. He said the warning was on there because E85 can damage engines. "Where did you hear that?" we asked as innocently as we could. "The tow truck guy told me," he said, "apparently it burns too hot or something."

We straightened him out. Alcohol burns cooler than gasoline.

Anyway, with our tank full of E85, we drove up over the Cascade Mountains (in Washington State). No problems. The only thing that seemed different is that the car had a little *more* power than we were used to. This is not surprising. They use ethanol in the Indianapolis 500 because it is not only safer but also because it gives a car more horsepower (it's a higher-octane fuel than gasoline).

Other than that, we couldn't tell any difference. So our non-flex-fuel Prius went up a long grade to a high elevation burning E80 with no problems. This was incredible. We were so happy. Marc Rauch and David Blume were right!

After about 90 miles, we stopped at a rest area and when we got back on the road, the engine light came on.

Uh oh.

But we already knew this was a possibility. The car kept running fine. There wasn't really a problem. But the O2 sensor was detecting fewer emissions than expected, and the car's onboard computer thought something must be wrong.

So we decided on our trip to drive the Prius for a while with the engine light on. The car ran perfectly. When it was time to fill up, we put in one gallon of regular gasoline to see if that would make the light go off. Apparently that wasn't enough. So we filled up on regular gasoline. Still the light stayed on. We thought we were going to have to take it to the shop to get it reset or something.

But before we headed for home, the light went off. Now we use E85 all the time and let the engine light shine like a badge of courage. We took the risk and discovered we could *immediately* stop sending our fuel dollars to OPEC and we could give it instead to American farmers and American workers where it does some good for our economy and our air quality (ethanol produces fewer emissions that cause health problems).

Once in a while when we get nervous about it, we fill the tank with gasoline just to see the engine light go off again. Maybe someday we'll put a conversion kit back on. Either way, we're not going back to petroleum.

The big money involved in the oil industry and their influence over governments, business, and the media may seem like too large a thing for you to have any effect on. But this week you'll be buying fuel for your car — you'll be choosing where to send your money. How things turn out is really *only* up to each of us. This is a vote that really counts. That tank of fuel you purchase either helps support the status quo or helps us reach a different kind of future. It's up to you.

Americans were enamored and inspired by the Arab Spring uprisings, and yet we feel powerless at home against political cronyism, oil money bribes (political contributions, weapons contracts, invitations to sit on the boards of corporations, etc.) and the overwhelming power and influence of the oil industry.

And yet, just like the individual people in Egypt, Syria and Libya, we can just as easily — far *more* easily — coordinate our efforts here to cut off the money to the oil industry, and we can begin immediately.

And since the United States is the biggest consumer of oil in the world, we can set a global trend right here and now.

When you buy E85, the money will probably go to an American. It will not go to any member of OPEC. You will be directly helping to break the monopoly of the illegal, immoral, unfair cartel.

People can disagree on what is the best fuel, but that doesn't really matter as much as you might think. We can all agree that competition is better than a monopoly. Right now, *today* we can pour our money into the only alternative there is — E85 — and make it the thin edge of a big wedge that opens the market for more and more alternatives to gasoline. The more the merrier. But we can start hammering in the wedge right now with E85. Make sure your car can burn it. That's step one.

2. Locate ethanol fuel stations and use them. Several web sites help you locate ethanol stations in your vicinity:

E85fuel.com

E85vehicles.com

ChooseEthanol.com

Or you can call the Department of Energy at 877.337.3463

You can also get an app for your smart phone that will locate ethanol stations. The Renewable Fuels Association offers a free Flex-Fuel Station Locator application that works great.

Once you've converted your car, find your nearest ethanol station and do your best to never buy gasoline again.

As soon as this movement begins to gain momentum, it's possible (likely?) that OPEC will lower the world price of oil to undercut its alcohol competition. If this happens — even if gasoline becomes cheaper than alcohol — I urge you to *keep buying alcohol fuels*. Keep those providers in business. Help keep those industries growing. Keep your money helping the poor and oppressed around the world, helping our economy, helping the environment, and helping your engine. And convince everyone you know to do the same. It will benefit us all in the long run.

Back in the 70s and 80s when organically grown vegetables first made their appearance in health food stores, and long before they made it to regular grocery stores, they were much more expensive than regular vegetables and they often didn't look as good. But many of us bought them anyway, knowing we were supporting a superior industry that was healthier for us and better for the environment, and we knew if we kept supporting them, more farms would use organic methods and the price would eventually come down. This has come to pass.

We weren't just buying groceries, we were putting our money where our mouth was. We were looking beyond the short-term savings and investing in the future we wanted.

We need to have the same attitude about alcohol fuels. Don't succumb to the temptation of cheap gasoline. Stick to your principles. Think of the future.

If our flex fuel capabilities are scrapped because of temporarily cheap oil, we'll have to begin again when oil prices rise because ethanol plants will have closed, like they did in the 80s. Ethanol entrepreneurs will have gone bankrupt. It would be a foolish, short-sighted move. Let's *keep* putting our money where our mouth is, regardless of what happens to oil prices, and create so many competing fuels that it no longer matters what OPEC does.

Let's strip oil, once and for all, of its strategic status.

In their book, *Turning Oil Into Salt*, Anne Korin and Gal Luft define our problem with America's dependence on oil in a way that opens the possibility of a solution. People have identified the problem in different ways, and of course, the way a problem is defined affects how we solve it. Defining a problem incorrectly can produce pointless or even counterproductive "solutions."

For example, do we use too much oil? Is that the problem? Is that what leaves us economically vulnerable to OPEC? Or do we *import* too much oil? Is that the problem?

Our attempts to solve *those* problems have led nowhere because the problem we need to solve is oil's strategic status. What does that mean? In the introduction to their book, Luft and Korin write:

> This book argues that the threat oil dependence presents to our national and economic security is not a function of the amount of oil we consume or import. It is a function of oil's status as a strategic commodity. Oil's strategic status stems from its virtual monopoly over fuel for transportation, which underlies the global economy and our entire way of life. Without oil, food cannot travel from farm to plate, mail cannot reach its destination, raw materials cannot reach their factories and children cannot attend their schools.

They use salt as an analogy. Salt was once a strategic commodity because it was the primary way to preserve food. It was very important to every country to have enough salt. Without a steady and secure supply of salt, food could not be preserved and widespread starvation would become a real possibility. So *wars were fought* over the possession of salt sources, wars were lost because of a lack of salt, and colonies were established because of salt.

In 1800, Napoleon Bonaparte offered a large reward to anyone who could find another way of preserving food for armies on the march. He defined the problem correctly. He didn't call for a different form of salt or ask how to use less salt for preserving food or how to make their own salt from something they possessed in abundance. He asked for an alternative way of *preserving food*. The way he defined the problem changed the world.

Within a very short time Nicholas Appert came up a solution — he invented the first canning process, originally using a glass container. Eventually there were *many* innovations in food preservation including tin cans, refrigeration, freeze-drying, and on and on. There are so many different ways to preserve food now that nobody even thinks about it. Nobody worries about salt. Nobody cares where it comes from or whether they will have enough of it or whether we import too much foreign salt.

Salt lost its *strategic status*. We haven't stopped using salt for preserving food — pickling vegetables and curing meats, for example — it is still a valuable commodity. But no wars will be fought over salt any more. No economies will crash because of it.

The problem we now need to solve is *oil's* strategic status. With 95 percent of transportation vehicles running on nothing but oil, and with transportation as the foundation of the economy, oil has an extremely high strategic status. It is the most important commodity in the world.

But if there were *many* ways to fuel our vehicles, we could arrive at a place where we didn't really care where oil comes from or whether there will be enough. Nobody would worry about it because we would have an abundance of other forms of fuel, and maybe even an abundance of other forms of transportation that don't even require fuel (like electric cars, for example).

The most efficient, effective and fastest way to reach this state is to use the technologies and infrastructure already available to us — to use vehicles and facilities we already have, to use car manufacturing techniques we already use, to use liquid fuel delivery systems we already have (but to increase the number of different liquid fuels) — and to have fuels that come from different sources. We can begin today by locating and patronizing E85 stations wherever possible. Help the industry develop by redirecting your money from the oil industry to the alcohol fuel industry.

3. If there is no E85 fuel pump near you, urge your favorite gas station to carry it, and then get everyone you know to buy their fuel there.

Whenever you buy fuel, if the station doesn't carry E85, ask them to. Leave them some information about it. Ask to speak to the owner, and do your best persuasion job, pointing out any government incentives, the good PR exposure that could come from it, the new and growing market now being missed, the benefits to the American economy, world poverty, women's rights, national security, etc.

One of the most important missing ingredients required to strip oil of its strategic status is the *availability* of fuels other than gasoline. Ethanol stations are relatively abundant in the Midwest, but everywhere else, they are almost non-existent.

A company called "Propel" is trying to do something about it. The company is building fuel stations serving E85 and biodiesel, mostly on the West Coast for now.

The company is originally from Seattle, but they've temporarily stationed themselves in the city of Redwood because California gave them a grant to put in 75 stations. Propel is committed to at least 500 stations on the West Coast in the next five years.

Here's how they operate: They go to any individually-owned gas station, usually Shell or another chain (or convenience stores that carry gas to get people to stop and buy their snacks). Propel tells the station owner, "We'll come in, install everything, which takes three to four weeks construction time, and then we will take care of the Propel tanks and equipment."

The station owner doesn't have to do *anything*. Propel simply pays the station owner rent for the space they use. The Propel unit is 100% automated. They take cards only. So for the gas station or the convenience store owner, it's absolutely maintenance-free.

If you live on the West Coast, one way to get an E85 station near you is to encourage your local gas stations to rent a corner of their parking lot to Propel. Propel has some information on their web site you can give to your local station owner. As one gas station owner put it, "The main reason we installed the pumps is because people were asking about them, we wanted to give people more choices at the pump."

Other companies are doing something similar in other parts of the country.

There are so few FFVs on the road, it may not seem worth it to a station owner to add a pump. But on the other hand, because E85 pumps are even more rare proportionally than FFVs, a station can gain a competitive advantage over other stations in the area, often being the *only* station for that untapped market for miles around.

Promise the owner you'll use it regularly and that you'll try to convince all your friends and neighbors to use it too. Get an announcement of the new pump in the local paper if you can. Promise the station owner you will try to get that publicity. Whenever you see an FFV, tell the car's owner about the new station in town and why it's a great idea to stop using petroleum.

So this is a very practical action you can take for yourself, our country, and the environment: Urge a local station to install an E85 pump.

4. Educate your friends and family about fuel competition. Most people know almost nothing about alcohol fuels or how OPEC controls the world's oil price or what their gouging does to our country or what they're using their immense wealth for. This is one of the most important things you can do: Educate people about this issue. Sign up for free email updates at our web site, FillYourTankWithFreedom.com, and forward those updates to your friends and family.

People will sometimes have questions or objections. Take the time to answer them. Help people become educated about alcohol fuel. It's important that more people know about it.

And "like" our Facebook page, which you can find here: facebook.com/fillyourtankwithfreedom.

And share those posts on *your* Facebook page, to help raise awareness of this issue with your friends and family.

You can also find good articles and videos to share with your friends and family at SetAmericaFree.org, IAGS.org, EnergyVictory.net, and FuelFreedom.org.

In conversations, share what you're learning, share what you did to convert your car, share why you did it, why you're interested, and why this is so vital to our future. Loan your books and DVDs to your friends and family. Share online videos and articles with them.

The advantages of alcohol fuel won't likely be covered very well in major media outlets. And for years, people have been on the receiving end of what could legitimately be called a "well-funded disinformation campaign," so for many people it may take some considerable effort on your part to educate them because they've been so effectively turned against alcohol fuels.

Concentrate on the easy ones first. When you run out of those, you can work on the people among your friends and family who are more difficult to educate.

5. Convince all your friends and family to participate — to learn more, to educate their friends, and to convert their own cars. Once they understand what it's about, encourage them to participate. The most likely way anyone will find out about the value of fuel competition is through someone they personally know. Most politicians are reluctant to get on oil's bad side, and with oil's influence on the media, informative programs that don't mislead on this issue are few and far between. Personal relationships are our best hope.

So *please* take the time and make the effort to help everyone you know understand the value and urgency of fuel competition. Tell them everything you know, and as you learn more, tell them about it. And infect them with the *urgency* of the issue. Speed is important here. Speed is vital. Tell them what you're doing, urge them to do it too, and offer to help.

6. Buy multiple copies of these books and share them with your friends:

> *Turning Oil Into Salt* by Gal Luft and Anne Korin
>
> *Petropoly* by Anne Korin and Gal Luft
>
> *The Forbidden Fuel* by Hal Bernton, William Kovarik and Scott Sklar
>
> *Energy Victory* by Robert Zubrin
>
> *Alcohol Can Be a Gas* by David Blume

Sustainable Ethanol by Jeffrey and Adrian Goettemoeller

And the one in your hands.

And get the DVD, *Freedom*, by Josh and Rebecca Tickell and share it with your friends too. This documentary might be the best tool we have for awakening others to the potential impact of fuel competition in America. It is interesting, entertaining, and educational. It's easy to share and it might be worth the trouble to buy several copies and keep them circulating among your family and friends until you are all burning E85 in your cars.

George Bernard Shaw wrote, "This is the true joy in life, the being used for a purpose recognized by yourself as a mighty one; the being a force of nature instead of a feverish selfish clod of ailments and grievances complaining that the world will not devote itself to making you happy. I am of the opinion that my life belongs to the whole community and as long as I live it is my privilege to do for it whatever I can. I want to be thoroughly used up when I die, for the harder I work, the more I live. I rejoice in life for its own sake. Life is no 'brief candle' to me. It is sort of a splendid torch which I have a hold of for the moment, and I want to make it burn as brightly as possible before handing it over to future generations."

We've been looking for a mighty purpose for a long time, and we've finally found it: fuel competition. It will create so many positive benefits for America and for the world, and so few negative consequences, it is

140

astonishing. But it will not happen on its own quickly enough. The cause needs our help. Each of us.

The one thing this mighty purpose needs most is more people to find out that fuel competition is possible and that it will do a world of good for America and for humanity. Please do everything you can to help spread the word.

7. Every time an open fuel standard is proposed in Congress or your state legislature, call your elected officials and urge them to support it.

If you don't hear back from your elected official, do a follow-up call a week later. You have a right to hear back from them.

If you're willing to do more, get to know the official's staff member responsible for the bill, and establish a relationship with that person, sending information and visiting in person when the staff is in town.

And when there is a town hall meeting, go and participate. You can find more actions you can take at OpenFuelStandard.org. The fastest way to fuel competition is a national open fuel standard.

By a similar mandate, we added seatbelts to our cars and saved untold thousands of lives. We can mandate all cars become flex fuel vehicles and save the economic lives of hundreds of millions (or billions) of people worldwide. In a very real way, breaking oil's monopoly over transportation fuel will save the world.

An open fuel standard would mean the end of the petroleum-only standard, which the world has been stuck with since the early twentieth century. It means the end of a one-fuel economy and the beginning of a free market for transportation fuel.

As you already know, even though many excellent fuels are available that cost less and burn cleaner than gasoline, our cars are not warranted to burn these fuels in our engines. An open fuel standard would change this. It would say that a car cannot be sold that could perpetuate oil's monopoly. Gas-only cars would be a thing of the past.

With only a few small tweaks to the manufacture of a car, it could easily be capable of burning methanol, ethanol, butanol, and gasoline — in any combination or proportion. Each car would become a platform upon which fuels could compete.

The repercussions of an open fuel standard would be enormous. When cars start rolling off assembly lines capable of burning multiple fuels, gasoline would finally have competition, with all the consequences we've already covered — the economy, security, freedom, etc. — and you, the consumer, would finally have as much choice with your fuel as you do with everything else you buy.

8. If you own a home, you can make your own ethanol inexpensively. The basic process of making ethanol is very simple: Add carbohydrates and yeast to water. Let it sit until it stops fermenting. Then distill out the alcohol.

It is not difficult and it is legal.

At least one company is making it very easy to do. Check out MicroFueler.com to learn more.

In David Blume's book, *Alcohol Can Be a Gas*, he tells you everything you need to know about it, including even how to grow the crops and how to make a still. But several companies make and sell complete stills online:

RainierDistillers.com
CopperMoonshineStills.com
MileHiDistilling.com
FerroMit.com
SustainableTechSys.com
Amphora-Society.com

Most of us have come to think fuel production and delivery is the job of large companies. But ethanol production lends itself very well to small-scale operations, which is better for our national economic stability.

One of the primary reasons small-scale production by large numbers of people fits so well with ethanol is that alcohol is essentially *solar* power. Using the power of the sun, plants assemble water and CO_2 into carbohydrates. Yeast turns it into fuel.

Sunshine is not concentrated anywhere. So fuel production is most efficient when it is not concentrated anywhere either, but made and used near where it falls. I mean, why burn fuel transporting fuel (or fuel feedstocks) if you don't have to?

Besides that, the more widespread the sources of our fuel, the less vulnerable we are to any kind of event that could lead to a fuel crisis.

If nothing else, making your own fuel could be a hobby that saves you money. If you are making your own fuel and you have a surplus, you can share it with your neighbors. You and a friend might split the costs of an ethanol still, share the work and share the fuel.

You can find some excellent information about making your own fuel at this Yahoo group:

http://tech.groups.yahoo.com/group/alcoholfuel/

You simply need to get a "small fuel producer" permit from the US Alcohol and Tobacco Tax and Trade Bureau. You can download the PDF form here:

http://www.ttb.gov/forms/f511074.pdf

Two copies of the application should be sent to the TTB National Revenue Center. The address is:

Alcohol and Tobacco Tax and Trade Bureau
National Revenue Center
550 Main Street, Suite 8002
Cincinnati, Ohio 45202

Tel. 1-855-882-7665
Email: ttbquestions@ttb.gov

Permits are free, and entitle you to make up to 10,000 gallons of ethanol fuel at home for personal use per year. For more information, check out:

http://www.ttb.gov/industrial/alcohol-fuel-plants.shtml

http://journeytoforever.org/ethanol.html

9. Demand first-rate cars from your favorite car company. Boycott second-rate (gasoline-only) cars. Only buy flex fuel cars from now on.

There are very few differences between flex fuel and gasoline-only cars. The fuel lines are a little better in flex fuel cars. Maybe.

Robert Zubrin, who is an accomplished engineer, did an experiment on his car, a 2007 Chevy Cobalt (a non-flex-fuel vehicle) and in the process discovered some interesting things. He wanted to run his car on methanol, which is legal to burn for fuel, but illegal to sell in America (at over a 5.4% concentration). To make his regular, non-flex-fuel car capable of burning methanol, he had to replace one part — a fuel pump seal. The seal that came with the car was made of Viton, which methanol would dissolve. The new seal he installed was made out of a material called "Buna-N." The new part cost him forty-one cents.

Other than that, the only thing he had to do to his car was adjust the Engine Control Unit software. The computer onboard his car was the same computer used in flex fuel cars, although his car was not flex fuel. But the software that would allow the car to be a flex fuel car was *disabled*. Zubrin wrote, "Currently, all new gasoline-powered cars sold in the U.S. are flex-fuel cars, but only about 5 percent are being sold as such. The rest are being marketed with their flex-fuel capability disabled by their manufacturers."

Why would a car company disable a feature? If the car is capable of burning multiple fuels, why wouldn't a car company just leave it? Why *remove* a capability? Zubrin suggests one possible reason: Many oil companies are part owners in many car companies. For example, the sovereign wealth fund of Qatar (an OPEC nation) owns 17 percent of Volkswagen, the largest car company in the world. They have a potentially controlling interest. And they own 10 percent of Porsche.

This is not an isolated case. Various OPEC members have large investments in many car companies — Saab, Chrysler, Fiat, Mercedes.

"What about the two biggest American auto companies, GM and Ford?" asks Robert Zubrin. "The dominant positions in these companies are held by major Wall Street firms whose collective energy holdings exceed $700 billion. Thus, while the $9 billion these funds have invested in GM and the $24 billion placed in Ford are of great weight to the auto companies, the funds themselves are far more concerned about protecting their investments in oil."

But as consumers we can certainly demand only the best fuel lines and only the best fuel injector program for any car we buy. Carmakers will eventually see the light (or lose business). Flex fuel cars don't cost any more than gas-only cars — at least they don't cost any more to *you*. There is some controversy about whether or not it costs the *automaker* more money to manufacture. GM says making a flex fuel car adds $70 to production costs, which of course is not much compared to the cost of a car, but it doesn't get passed on to you anyway. Choose to have a choice at the pump.

The oil industry propaganda makes a big deal out of ethanol being less energy dense than gasoline. But apparently it is a misleading comparison. People who test it find that the fuel mileage for E85 is much better than could be expected from the difference in energy density. One car engineer explained it by saying that ethanol generates less waste heat to be dumped into the radiator. Gasoline has a higher BTU but that is a measurement of *heat*, and heat does not help the car move forward.

It also makes a difference whether the car engine is optimized for gasoline and can also burn E85, or whether it's optimized for E85 and can also burn gasoline. For example, in a higher compression engine, E85 does better. More and more cars will be optimized for E85 in the future. Get one of those when you can.

10. Buy plug-in flex-fuel hybrids when they become available. This is the ultimate OPEC-free car. Plug it in and fill it with alcohol fuel. OPEC gets nothing. Ford, GM, and Lotus are working on bringing such cars to the public.

11. If you have a diesel engine, run it on biodiesel. No conversion is necessary. It can run on biodiesel today. You can also use waste cooking oil in your diesel engine with no other processing than filtering out the chunks. Go to your local diner or restaurant or hamburger joint and ask for their used deep fryer oil. Find out when they change the oil and pick it up from them on those days, and you will have *free* fuel. You can just filter it and put it straight into your unaltered diesel car and drive. This doesn't require any conversion. You get free fuel. OPEC gets nothing.

I had heard about this, but I was skeptical until I watched a MythBusters episode in which the hosts (Adam Savage and Jamie Hyneman) tried to find out if the claim had any validity.

It did.

They went to a fast-food restaurant, took away a bucket of used fryer oil that the store was going to throw away (restaurants cannot keep using the same oil to deep fry food, or it starts to taste bad). The Myth Busters guys filtered out the little particles of food, and put it in their unaltered diesel car. It ran perfectly.

12. Support the Fuel Freedom Foundation. Founded by two successful software entrepreneurs, the organization is working to get outdated regulations changed (the EPA's restrictive regulations for methanol, for example).

Its mission statement says it is a "non-partisan initiative dedicated to breaking our oil addiction with cheaper, cleaner, American-made replacement fuels by removing barriers to fuel competition."

This is a worthy organization to support. Donate to them. Find them on Facebook or Google+ and share their posts with others. Share their articles and videos with people. Look them up at fuelfreedom.org.

13. Get this book carried by your local library. Usually libraries have a form you can fill out to request new books. When this book is available on a library shelf, more people will learn about fuel choice and fuel competition.

14. Get T-Shirts, bumper stickers, and car magnets that advertise fuel competition, fuel choice, and flex fuel cars. There are several companies that allow you to make your own customized products like this. CafePress.com, Signazon.com and VistaPrint.com all do this. Raise public awareness of these ideas in every way possible.

Create business cards with a short list of web links where people can get more information, so in your conversations with people, when they show some interest, you can hand them the card and urge them to get more information, sign up for updates, etc. Make it easy for people to take the next step. And take advantage of any kind of interest someone has while it is fresh in their minds by always having a couple of these business cards with you to hand out. The best one for business cards is VistaPrint.com.

15. Join Alcoholics Unanimous online and invite your friends. It is an online social network for fans of David Blume's book, *Alcohol Can Be a Gas*. There are different sub-groups within the network for people working on different kinds of projects, like making their own fuel or converting their cars. And there are also sub-groups for different geographical areas, so you can connect to people doing things with ethanol in your city or town. If you'd like to communicate with fans of ethanol, join at ACBAGnetwork.ning.com.

16. Show the film, Freedom, at any meeting you attend regularly (church group, service club, whatever). Or show one of our short YouTube videos (one is titled, *What is an Open Fuel Standard?*) and have a discussion about it. You could give them a presentation about the Open Fuel Standard or fuel competition in general.

17. Make a school project or presentation about the Open Fuel Standard or fuel competition. Encourage your kids to do a school project about it. More education on the fundamentals and consequences of fuel competition are desperately needed.

18. Contact your local Clean Cities organization and see what you can do to help them or what they can do to help you. Clean Cities is a national organization with over a hundred coalitions. Most people in the United States live inside the boundaries of at least one Clean Cities coalition. They can bring together resources to help fleets convert to non-petroleum vehicles, help you get an ethanol pump in your town, find funding for projects that help break the oil monopoly, etc. Visit their web site to find out more:

http://www1.eere.energy.gov/cleancities/

Do these simple, practical things and you will cause a whole slew of positive effects in the world, in America, in your local area, and even in your car. You might even be happier.

Filling Our Own Tank
With Freedom

This chapter was written by me, Klassy, the mechanic in the family, shortly after we filled our tank with freedom for the first time. We already had a very fuel efficient car, but it still burned gasoline. Once we learned what OPEC is doing to our national economy, we knew we had to do something about it. Here's what I wrote:

We converted our car and it feels great! We broke free. It's been a long time since I did something that made me so happy. We just filled up our tank with E85. For the first time in my life, I had a choice at the pump and I got to buy American-made alcohol, which means OPEC got next to nothing from me.

We wanted a flex fuel car because dependence on foreign oil threatens our national security. Our economy depends on a fuel controlled by men who seek to rule the world. Sounds so dramatic, I know, but it's still true. The military understands this. Nearly every military facility, at least around here, has an E85 station.

I think one way to help others get the message about stripping oil of its strategic status is by actually changing our own world as a demonstration of what needs to be done; and maybe even more importantly, to show people how good it feels to own a flex fuel car. And I'm here to tell you, it feels good to have choice.

It may seem silly to talk about the emotions of all this, but that has been the biggest shift for me. Now it doesn't bring me down every time I fill the tank. In fact, now when I fill the tank it makes me happy! In a world where I often feel helpless, having done something that makes me feel in charge gives me a kind of strength, a sense of power. I actually *did* something real and concrete to stop the flow of money from the free world to OPEC. It gives me a real sense of satisfaction. I stopped a terrible thing from happening in the world. I stopped funding those who hate freedom, especially women's freedom.

I could have asked my mechanic to install the conversion kit, but I wanted to do it myself, just to see how hard it was. I had watched some video clips that made it look pretty easy. One showed two young boys doing it, ages thirteen and nine! Another showed a pretty woman installing it in maybe five minutes. I saw another one of a movie star who did it in seven minutes.

"If they can do it," I thought, "I can do it."

When I looked around online for conversion kits I met a great group of guys. I called and talked with Ian

Crawford from AlcoholCanBeAGas.com and Jonny Energy from JonnyEnergy.com and Don Althoff from FlexFuelUS.com. They not only answered my questions, they offered to let me call them when it was time to install it so they could coach me through it. Now that's service!

We decided to buy our kit from the good folks at AlcoholCanBeAGas.com because they've been around since the 1970's and David Blume and Ian Crawford know a lot about alcohol fuel.

When it came time to install the conversion kit (which I did without any coaching on the phone), nothing seemed to go right. I needed a 10mm socket and I couldn't find one. So I found a neighbor who works on cars and he lent me one.

I needed the socket because in our car the air filter housing prevents access to the fuel injectors. But it was pretty easy to get the housing off. Then I could see the fuel injectors. But then I dropped a little plastic part down between the radiator and the grill. I couldn't reach it from above. I couldn't reach it from below. Grrrr. It took some time, but I eventually was able to get that part out. Then I was back to the installation.

The conversion kit is a little black box about the size of a long pack of cigarettes. There's a computer inside. I attached it to a good spot inside the engine compartment with some Velcro strips. There are wires that go from the conversion box to each one of the fuel injectors. The actual installation is pretty straightforward. At the end of each wire there's a little connector. All you have to do is unplug the wire that goes into the fuel injector and plug it into the converter connector and then plug the converter wire into the fuel injector. We have four cylinders, so I did this four times. Then when the car's computer sends a signal to the fuel injector to inject fuel, the signal goes to the converter box first, which adds the appropriate adjustment so the car can use E85 as well as gasoline.

That's it. Oh, then I used some of those little plastic jobbers to bind up the wires all nice and neat and out of the way. Then I put the air filter housing back in place. Three bolts. Done. And even with my lack of tools, and my clumsiness, and having never installed one before, and even though I didn't do it in seven minutes, the whole thing, start-to-finish was less than a half hour. And I didn't even hurt my manicure.

The car started right up. No engine light. All the gauges work the same. We drove around. No difference. Slick! I felt more than a bit smug that I could now say I did it myself. Just to complete the process, we bought an emblem online that says "flex fuel" and put it on our car. Big smile.

But the real thrill was at the pump. That was truly one of the happiest moments I've had in awhile. I have a sense of ownership of my life I didn't have before. All the times I've bought gasoline knowing I was paying Wahhabi fanatics who hate my rights as a woman, all the times I felt like a victim to a horrible situation, all the times I felt defeated and beaten by the system, all that stopped.

I hope some day soon an open fuel standard will become law, but even if it does, that won't change *my* car. We need to pass an OFS bill but we also need to convert the cars already on the road. And there are about 240 million cars in America that can only burn gasoline. Nearly all those could be easily converted in less than a half hour and for less than a hundred dollars a cylinder.

What are you waiting for? All of us can be driving flex fuel cars right now. And the more cars we convert and the faster we do it, the quicker we can feel safe and secure as a nation.

As my dad used to say: Put your money where your mouth is.

At a time when we often feel like there's nothing we can do, here's something we can do. Every car that only burns gasoline contributes to OPEC and helps cruel governments repress women. Every car you convert not only buys your freedom of choice at the pump, it helps weaken those repressive governments. And all the money that used to flow out of our free world will now stay and help us build better lives.

With one simple, practical action, I have accomplished a small part of what we need and want — national security, economic vitality, environmental health, and energy independence. A better world. And that feels good.

Made in the USA
San Bernardino, CA
29 January 2014